whip

expert cakes
meringues • soufflés • batters
ice creams • desserts • sauces

maggie mayhew

MQP
MQ Publications Ltd

Copyright © 2001 MQ Publications Limited
Text copyright © 2001 Maggie Mayhew

Project editor: Nicola Birtwisle
Text editor: Coralie Dorman
Designer: Elizabeth Ayer
Photography: Janine Hosegood
Stylist: Vanessa Kellas

Published by MQ Publications Limited
12 The Ivories, 6–8 Northampton Street, London N1 2HY
Tel: 020 7359 2244 / Fax: 020 7359 1616
email: mail@mqpublications.com

ISBN: 1 84072 257 6

Printed and bound in England by Butler & Tanner Ltd

MQ 10 9 8 7 6 5 4 3 2 1

Kitchen equipment kindly supplied by Gill Wing Cookshop,
190 Upper Street, London N1 1RQ
Tel: 020 7226 5392

contents

introduction 6

equipment 10

cakes 14

meringues 48

ice creams and other desserts 68

soufflés 88

batters 106

sauces 126

index 143

introduction

Whipping isn't just for cream and meringues. There are lots of things you can do with this magical technique. To whip, or whisk, means to incorporate air into a mixture to give a frothy or stiffened consistency. Cakes and soufflés just wouldn't exist without air, as they depend on it to help them rise and to improve their texture.

When making sauces, on the other hand, the whisk and the whipping process are useful for different reasons. In roux sauces the technique lets you cook the sauce over a higher heat, making it less likely to form lumps. Rapid whisking also helps reduce the risk of the sauce burning on the bottom of the pan. When making mayonnaise-style sauces, the whisk combines fat- and water-based ingredients to make an emulsion with a stable, creamy consistency.

The most basic piece of whipping equipment is, unsurprisingly, the whisk. They're available in many shapes and sizes, from simple balloon whisks to hand-held electric models. In some cases a fork can be used to achieve the same result but this will require a much faster wrist action.

The best way to whip by hand is to hold the whisk loosely between the thumb and forefinger, like a pencil, allowing the handle to rest on the side of the hand. Then whip with a circular action from the wrist, as lightly and quickly as you can, to allow pockets of air to become trapped within the mixture.

the basics: whipping cream

It's important to start with chilled cream – either double or whipping cream – and use a cold bowl, preferably ceramic, stainless steel or glass. The best style of whisk to use is a balloon, hand-held electric or old-fashioned hand-held rotary whisk. Whip quickly to begin with until the cream starts to thicken and becomes the consistency of custard. Now's the time to reduce the whipping speed so you don't overwhip. If you continue whipping for a short while, the cream will begin to hold its shape but will drop easily from a spoon. At this stage it is of spooning consistency. It will have some texture but won't hold its shape for long.

If you whip for a few seconds more, the cream should start to hold its shape and will have a glossy sheen. Once you get to this stage, the cream is perfect for serving, as it will thicken slightly on standing or piping.

Make sure you don't over-whip your cream. If you keep whipping past this stage, the cream will form stiff peaks and become too thick and buttery in texture. If over-whipped cream is left at room temperature it may even separate out into curds and whey.

the basics: whisking egg whites

Whisking is a vital process in the making of a meringue. When egg whites are whisked, they increase their volume and become frothy, light and airy. They will achieve a better volume if they are left at room temperature for a couple of hours, and not used cold, straight from the refrigerator.

Use a balloon or egg whisk for the best volume and texture, but if you are not used to whisking by hand, or speed is of the essence, an electric hand-held or tabletop whisk will be fine. Separate the eggs, allowing the whites to drop into a grease-free, non-reactive bowl. If any egg yolk falls in with it, remove before starting to whisk. The easiest way to do this is to use one of the broken eggshells: for some quirky reason the yolk is attracted to the shell. Whisk quickly and lightly in an even, steady movement. The egg whites will become frothy but still liquid.

If you continue whisking past this stage the whites will become stiff but smooth. This is the stiff peak stage, when sugar or syrup can be added. A good way to check if this stage has been reached is to tip the bowl. If the egg whites begin to slide out of the bowl they need further whisking.

If sugar is to be added, lightly sprinkle it over the top, a spoonful at a time, whisking well in between each addition. When the egg whites are very stiff and glossy the remaining sugar or ingredients can be folded in gently with a metal spoon to prevent knocking out the air.

Now you've learned the basics, it's time to put them into practice. Shown on the next four pages are all the pieces of equipment you'll ever need.

equipment

twirl whisk This manual whisk is very flexible and useful for working around the entire base of the bowl or pan. Great for preventing lumps in sauces.

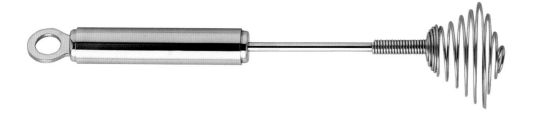

hand-held rotary whisk The all-time reliable kitchen favourite, this whisk is really easy to use.

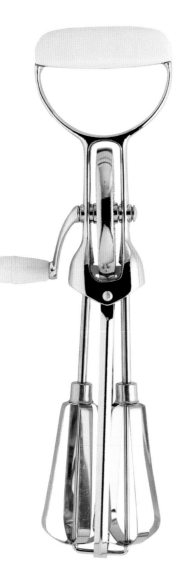

spiral whisk Ideal for whisking sauces in shallow dishes and for getting into the corners of a bowl.

egg whisk More wires than an ordinary balloon whisk make this good for aerating egg-based sauces and egg whites for meringue.

sauce and dressing whisk This small whisk is perfect for making tiny quantities. Very light and easy to use in smaller containers.

balloon whisk The classic whisk, this can be used for aerating both light and heavy ingredients. It's especially good for cream and butter sauces.

electric hand-held whisk This good all-rounder gives you more control than a tabletop mixer and is far easier to use than a balloon whisk.

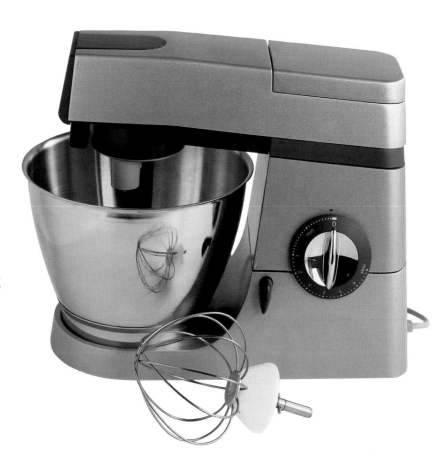

tabletop mixer These super-powerful tabletop machines are great for cake mixes and for making meringues. Only for the serious cook, as they can be a little expensive.

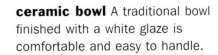

ceramic bowl A traditional bowl finished with a white glaze is comfortable and easy to handle.

copper bowl A non-reactive copper bowl makes your meringue more stable and easier to work with.

glass bowl This is a good general mixing bowl, suitable for all ingredients and heavy enough to sit firmly on the work top.

melamine bowl Practical, cheap and unbreakable, plastic-based bowls often have a non-slip rubber base.

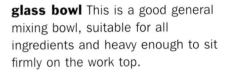

stainless steel bowl Stainless steel is ideal for all food preparation as it is resistant to food acids and colours.

cakes

cakes There are as many differerent ways of making cakes as there are cakes to make, but they're all based on the same core technique – whipping or whisking. The method and quantities of ingredients are then subtly altered to make the cake drier, moister or lighter. Cake-making really is a fine art! In this chapter we show you the basic methods to make some of the most popular types of cake, plus some delicious variations.

american sponge the basic method The

technique of whipping or whisking is essential in the making of American sponge cakes. Try this traditional method to make a light, airy-textured cake.

step 1 Separate the eggs and put the yolks into a large, roomy mixing bowl and add sugar. Whisk together using a hand-held electric whisk until the egg yolks are thick and pale yellow.

step 2 Remove the beaters and wash them. In a separate large mixing bowl, and with the clean beaters, start whisking the egg whites, moving the beaters all round the bowl.

step 3 Keep on whisking the egg whites – you can use a balloon whisk instead of the electric whisk if preferred – until they reach the stiff peak stage.

step 4 Gradually whisk in the sugar, sprinkling it over the surface 1 tablespoon at a time, and making sure it is thoroughly incorporated before adding the next, whisking until stiff and glossy.

step 5 Sift the flour over the egg yolks in the first bowl then fold it in carefully, using a spatula or large metal spoon. Finally, fold in the egg whites.

American whipped sponge cake

3 large eggs, separated • 100g caster sugar • 1 tsp vanilla extract • ¼ tsp cream of tartar • 50g plain flour, sifted • pinch of salt • 300ml double cream • 100g fresh strawberries • icing sugar, for dusting

SERVES 6–8

This traditional American light-as-a-feather sponge cake recipe is flavoured with vanilla and is perfect served with fruit and cream.

1. Preheat the oven to 180°C/350°F/gas 4. Line the base of a 20cm springform tube tin.

2. Whisk the egg yolks and 4 tablespoons of the sugar together until thick and pale. Whisk in the vanilla extract.

3. Whisk the egg whites and cream of tartar until they are stiff. Gradually whisk in the remaining sugar until stiff and glossy. Sift the flour and salt over the egg yolks and fold in with a quarter of the whisked egg white. Fold in the remaining egg white.

4. Spoon the mixture into the prepared tin and bake until golden and the top springs back when pressed lightly, 30–40 minutes. Turn the tin upside down on a wire rack and let cool, 30 minutes. Run a knife around the inside of the tin then turn the cake out onto a wire rack. Turn right side up and let cool completely.

5. Whip the cream to soft peaks and pile onto the cake. Spread over the top and sides and decorate with small whole or halved strawberries. Dust the top with icing sugar before serving.

Candied fruit cassata

6 tbsp sweet Marsala · 500g fresh ricotta · 100g icing sugar, sifted · 75g plain chocolate, finely chopped · 100g chopped mixed glacé fruits · 75g toasted flaked almonds, chopped · For the sponge fingers · 100g plain flour · 4 large eggs, separated · 100g caster sugar · 1 tsp vanilla extract · icing sugar for dusting

SERVES 6

A cassata, or 'little case' in Italian, is traditionally made in a loaf tin, but a bowl or straight-sided mould may also be used. A slightly drier, closer-textured sponge finger is needed for this recipe, and to this end, the mixture contains a higher proportion of flour. Shop-bought sponge fingers can also be used – if you do this, miss out steps 1–4.

1. To make the sponge fingers, grease and flour two baking sheets. Preheat the oven to 180°C/350°F/gas 4. Sift the flour into a bowl.

2. Put the egg yolks into a heatproof bowl. Put over a saucepan of simmering water and whisk with half the sugar until they reach the ribbon stage (see page 24). Whisk in the vanilla extract.

3. In a separate bowl, whisk the egg whites until they form stiff peaks. Add the remaining sugar and continue to whisk until they form a glossy meringue.

4. Use a large metal spoon to gently fold the meringue and then the sifted flour into the whisked egg yolks. Spoon the mixture into a piping bag fitted with a plain 2cm nozzle and quickly pipe 11cm lengths of mixture in lines on the prepared baking sheets. Dust the tops with icing sugar and bake until pale golden and just firm to the touch, 15–18 minutes. Cool on a wire rack.

5. To assemble, line a 1.2 litre soufflé dish with clingfilm. Cut half the sponge fingers into petal shapes to fit into the bottom. Dip into the Marsala and arrange in the base. Cut the remaining fingers to fit around the sides and then dip each in the Marsala and arrange around the sides of the dish.

6. Mix together the remaining ingredients and spoon into the dish. Top with any leftover pieces of sponge finger and add any remaining Marsala. Cover and chill overnight. Turn out, dust with icing sugar and serve with cream.

Coffee, maple and pecan sponge cake

75g plain flour • pinch salt • 40g unsalted butter • 3 large eggs • 75g caster sugar • 1 tsp coffee and chicory essence • 1 tbsp hot water • ½ tsp vanilla extract • For the icing • 175g butter • 100g icing sugar • 4 tbsp maple syrup • 1 tsp coffee and chicory essence • 1 tbsp hot water • 8 pecan halves to decorate

SERVES 6–8

In this method, whole eggs are whisked with sugar over hot water until the ribbon stage has been reached. The standard ratio is 2 tablespoons sugar and 4 tablespoons plain flour for each egg used. Melted butter is added to this cake mixture to increase richness and also to improve its keeping properties.

1. Grease and line a 20cm round cake tin. Preheat the oven to 180ºC/350ºF/gas 4. Sift the flour and salt together three times and set aside. Melt the butter.

2. Break the eggs into a large bowl and add the sugar. Put over a pan of simmering water and whisk together until they form the ribbon stage (see page 24).

3. Whisk in the coffee and chicory essence and the vanilla extract. Sift the flour over the eggs in three batches, drizzling a little butter around the bowl in between each batch and folding in. Discard any white, milky sediment left at the bottom of the saucepan.

4. Pour mixture into the prepared tin and bake until golden and the top springs back when pressed lightly, 25–30 minutes. Let cool in the tin 2–3 minutes then turn out onto a wire rack to cool completely.

5. For the icing, beat the butter and icing sugar together until smooth. Gradually beat the coffee and chicory essence into the icing with the maple syrup until soft and smooth.

6. Cut the cake twice horizontally to make three layers and spread icing over each layer. Assemble the cake and spread the remaining icing around the sides and on top. Decorate with the pecan halves.

Chocolate and raspberry torte

50g plain flour · 4 tbsp cocoa powder · 40g unsalted butter · 3 large eggs ·
75g caster sugar · 425ml double cream · 4 tbsp orange liqueur · 175g fresh or frozen
raspberries · 1 tbsp icing sugar · 50g plain chocolate, grated

SERVES 6–8

This elegant gâteau makes a fantastic dessert as you can make it ahead and freeze to save time on the actual day.

1. Grease and line a 23cm round cake tin. Preheat the oven to 180°C/350°F/gas 4. Sift the flour and the cocoa together and melt the butter.

2. Break the eggs into a bowl and add the caster sugar. Place the bowl over a saucepan of hot water and whisk with an electric hand-held whisk until they reach the ribbon stage (see page 24).

3. In three batches, sift the flour and cocoa over the eggs and gently fold in, drizzling a little butter around the bowl in between each batch. Discard any white sediment at the bottom of the pan.

4. Pour into the prepared tin and bake until brown and the top springs back when pressed lightly, 20 minutes. Let cool in the pan 2–3 minutes then turn out onto a wire rack to cool completely.

5. For the filling, whip the cream and liqueur until the mixture forms soft peaks. Fold in the raspberries, sugar and chocolate.

6. Cut the cake through horizontally to make two layers. Line a 20cm springform tin with baking parchment and trim the cake to fit the base of the tin. Put one of the cake halves at the bottom. Pile in the raspberry cream and top with the remaining cake. Press down evenly and freeze until the filling is firm, 4 hours. Dust the top with cocoa then remove from the tin and serve in slices.

Swiss roll with lemon cream

**4 large eggs · 100g caster sugar, plus extra for dusting · 100g plain flour ·
For the filling · 250g mascarpone cheese · grated zest and juice of ½ lemon ·
2 tbsp fresh orange juice · 4 tbsp icing sugar**

SERVES 6

**A sponge finger batter (see page 20) can also be used
for Swiss rolls but won't give such a moist cake. Try jam,
butter cream or cream and fruit as alternative fillings.**

1. Preheat the oven to 220°C/425°F/gas 7. Grease and line a
23 x 33cm Swiss roll tin with baking parchment.

2. Whisk the eggs and sugar with a hand-held electric whisk in a
large bowl until thick and frothy and the beaters leave a trail when
lifted out of the mixture – this is called the ribbon stage.

3. Sift and fold in the flour in three batches. Pour the mixture into
the prepared tin and spread lightly into the corners. Bake until
golden and the top springs back when pressed, about 10 minutes.

4. While the cake is cooking, lay a sheet of baking parchment on a
work surface and sprinkle liberally with caster sugar.

5. Holding the lining paper and tin edges, turn the cake out onto
the paper. Peel the lining paper from the cake. Trim
off the edges from the cake and score a cut 1cm
in from one of the shorter ends. Roll up the cake
with baking parchment and let cool on a wire rack.

6. Beat the filling ingredients together. Carefully
unroll the cake and spread with filling. Roll up and
serve cut into slices.

5

6

Coconut and cherry Swiss roll

4 large eggs • 100g caster sugar, plus extra for dusting • 100g plain flour •
50g piece creamed coconut, finely shredded • For the filling • 150ml double cream •
2 tbsp kirsch • 225g pitted bottled cherries, drained

SERVES 6-8

Creamed coconut has a lovely flavour and is less granular than the dessicated sort. Use fresh cherries when they are in season.

1. Preheat the oven to 220°C/425°F/gas 7. Grease and line a 23 x 33cm Swiss roll tin with baking parchment.

2. Whisk the eggs and caster sugar together in a large bowl with an electric hand-held whisk until they reach the ribbon stage (see page 24). Sift the flour over the mixture in three batches and fold in gently after each addition with a large metal spoon. Fold in the creamed coconut with the last batch of flour.

3. Pour into the prepared tin and spread lightly into the corners. Bake until golden brown and the top springs back when pressed, 10 minutes. While the cake is cooking, lay a sheet of baking parchment on a work surface and sprinkle liberally with caster sugar.

4. Holding the lining paper and tin edges, turn the cake out onto the sugar-dusted paper. Peel the lining paper from the cake and trim the edges. Score a cut 2.5cm in from one of the shorter ends.

5. Place a sheet of baking parchment over the surface and roll up from the scored end with the parchment inside (see page 25). Cool the Swiss roll on a wire rack.

6. Whip the cream and kirsch together until the mixture forms soft peaks. Unroll the cake and fill with cream and cherries. Roll up and serve sliced.

Middle Eastern orange cake

2 small oranges • 5 eggs • 175g light muscovado sugar • 225g ground almonds • 50g plain flour • 1 tsp baking powder • 2 tbsp flaked almonds • icing sugar, for dusting

SERVES 8–10

To flavour this moist and delicious cake, a whole orange, including the pith and peel, is used. This gives it a really intense citrus taste that's perfect to serve as a dessert with crème fraiche or whipped cream.

1. Put the oranges in a saucepan and cover with water. Bring to the boil, cover and simmer until the oranges are really soft, 1½ hours. Drain and let cool. Halve the oranges and remove the pips then purée in a food processor or blender. Measure 300ml of the pulp and discard the rest.

2. Grease and line a 23cm round cake tin. Preheat the oven to 180°C/350°F/gas 4. Whisk the eggs and caster sugar together in a large bowl until they are thick and foamy and the mixture leaves a ribbon trail when the whisk is lifted (see page 24).

3. Fold the orange pulp into the eggs with the almonds, flour and baking powder. Pour into the prepared tin, scatter the almonds over the surface and bake 1 hour. Test for doneness by inserting a skewer into the centre; it should come out clean if cooked.

4. Allow to cool in the tin 10 minutes then remove from the tin and peel off the lining paper. Dust the top with icing sugar. Cool on a wire rack or serve warm with whipped cream.

creamed sponge cake the basic method

These are notorious for separating, so make sure all the ingredients are at room temperature before you start, which helps. Here butter and sugar are whipped or 'creamed' together until light and fluffy to incorporate plenty of air. Add the eggs one at a time, getting yet more air into the cake mixture. This is the key to its success. The flour is gently folded in which stops the cake from toughening. Proportions are generally equal weights but this can vary slightly.

step 1 Whisk the butter and sugar with an electric hand-held whisk or a balloon whisk in a large mixing bowl until they are pale and fluffy and no longer grainy.

step 2 Break the eggs into a separate bowl. Using a balloon whisk, whisk the eggs to break them up slightly. This makes them easier to add to the rest of the mixture.

step 3 A little at a time, gradually whisk the beaten eggs into the butter and sugar mixture in the first bowl. Make sure you whisk well after each addition of egg.

step 4 Sift over the flour and any other dry ingredients like ground nuts or cocoa powder. Fold into the mixture gently, with the electric whisk set at a slow speed, until combined.

Orange and almond sponge cake

175g butter • 175g caster sugar • 3 eggs • 150g self-raising flour • 50g ground almonds • a few drops almond extract • **For the icing** • 300g full fat soft cheese • 2 tbsp fresh orange juice • 2 tsp grated orange zest • 100g icing sugar, sifted • toasted flaked almonds and orange zest to decorate

SERVES 6–8

This delicious moist sponge filled with cream cheese and flavoured with tangy oranges is great with morning coffee and is special enough for dessert too.

1. Grease and line the bases of two 20cm round sandwich tins. Preheat the oven to 190ºC/375ºF/gas 5. Whisk the butter and caster sugar with an electric hand-held whisk in a bowl until the mixture is pale and fluffy.

2. Whisk the eggs then gradually whisk into the butter and sugar mixture. Sift over the flour and almonds and add the almond extract. Fold into the mixture gently until combined.

3. Spoon the mixture into the tins and level the surfaces. Bake until golden and the centres of the cakes spring back when pressed lightly, 20–25 minutes.

4. Turn out of the tins and cool on a wire rack. Meanwhile make the icing. Beat the cream cheese in a bowl to soften. Add the orange juice and zest and icing sugar and beat until smooth and creamy.

5. Sandwich the cakes together with a little of the icing, and use a palette knife to spread the rest of the icing over the top. Scatter toasted flaked almonds and orange zest over the top to decorate.

Lemon and poppy seed pound cake

175g butter • 175g caster sugar • 3 eggs, beaten • 175g self-raising flour • 1 tbsp poppy seeds • 2 tsp grated lemon zest • For the syrup • 3 tbsp caster sugar • juice of 1 lemon

SERVES 6–8

This poppy seed cake is soaked with a tangy lemon syrup after it's been baked to give a really moist, delicious texture. It will keep well in an airtight container for up to a week.

1. Preheat the oven to 180°C/350°F/gas 4. Grease and base line a 900g loaf tin.

2. Whip the butter and sugar together until light and fluffy. Gradually whisk in the eggs a little at a time then fold in the flour, poppy seeds and lemon zest.

3. Turn the mixture into the prepared tin and bake until risen, golden and a skewer inserted into the centre comes out clean, 1¼–1½ hours. Remove the cake from the oven but leave in the tin.

4. To make the syrup, gently heat the sugar and lemon juice together until the sugar has dissolved. Bring to a boil then pour over the cake and let cool. Cut into slices to serve.

Devil's food cake with chocolate orange frosting

175g plain chocolate · 150g unsalted butter · 150g caster sugar · 6 large eggs, separated · 75g plain flour · 50g ground almonds · For the frosting · 200ml double cream · 200g plain chocolate · 2 tsp grated orange zest

SERVES 8

This is a real chocoholic's dream. Wickedly indulgent, rich and delicious, it combines the American sponge cake and creamed sponge cake methods.

1. Grease and line a 20cm round cake tin with baking parchment. Preheat the oven to 180°C/350°F/gas 4. Melt the chocolate for the cake in a bowl set over a pan of hot water. Cool slightly.

2. Meanwhile, beat the butter and half the sugar until creamy. Whisk in the melted chocolate then the egg yolks, one at a time.

3. Sift the flour and almonds together into a separate bowl. Whisk the egg whites in a separate bowl until stiff then gradually whisk in the remaining sugar. Stir half the egg whites into the chocolate mixture to loosen it slightly, then fold in the flour and almond mixture with the remaining egg white.

4. Spoon into the prepared tin and bake until a skewer inserted into the centre comes out clean, 50–60 minutes. Cool in the tin 10 minutes. Remove from the tin and cool completely on a wire rack.

5. To make the frosting, heat the cream in a saucepan until nearly boiling. Remove from the heat and stir in the chocolate until melted then stir in the orange zest. Keep stirring until the frosting thickens. Pour over the cake and spread evenly over the top and sides. Let the frosting set before dusting with icing sugar.

Double chocolate chunk brownies

**500g dark chocolate • 225g butter, diced • 1 tsp instant coffee powder •
1 tbsp hot water • 3 large eggs • 175g caster sugar • 1 tsp vanilla extract •
100g self-raising flour • 175g pecan nuts, broken into pieces**

MAKES 12 brownies

**It's important when making brownies that they are not
overcooked or they'll lose their characteristic delicious
gooey centre. Add any nuts you prefer, such as
macadamia or peanut.**

1. Preheat the oven to 190ºC/375ºF/gas 5. Grease and line a
20 x 30cm cake tin with baking parchment.

2. Chop 175g of the chocolate into chunks and set aside. Put the
rest in a bowl with the butter and melt slowly over a pan of hot
water. Stir until smooth then let cool. Meanwhile, dissolve the
coffee in the hot water.

3. Lightly whisk together the eggs, coffee, sugar and vanilla.
Gradually whisk in the chocolate and butter mixture then fold in the
flour, nuts and chocolate chunks. Pour into the prepared tin. Bake
until firm to the touch, 35–40 minutes.

4. Cool 5 minutes then cut into squares. Let cool in the tin before
removing from the lining paper.

Frosted lime tray-bake

225g butter, softened • 225g caster sugar • 225g self-raising flour • 1 tsp baking powder • 4 large eggs • 2 tsp grated lime zest • For the topping • finely pared zest of 2 limes and the juice of 3 limes • 100g granulated sugar

SERVES 6–8

This cake uses a simple all-in-one method. It's a quick method that doesn't allow as much air to be incorporated as the traditional creaming method. To overcome this, extra raising agent is added with the flour. The crunchy topping is just as delicious if you use lemon or orange juice in place of the lime. The secret is to pour it over while the cake is still hot so the juice soaks in and the sugar forms a crunchy topping as it cools.

1. Preheat the oven to 180°C/350°F/gas 4. Lightly grease and line a 18 x 28cm baking tin with baking parchment.

2. Measure all the ingredients into a bowl and whisk together until light and smooth. Turn the mixture into the prepared tin and spread over evenly.

3. Bake until the cake is well risen, golden and the top springs back when pressed lightly, 40 minutes.

4. Mix the topping ingredients together in a bowl. Remove the cake from the oven and pour over the sugar topping. Let cool in the tin then turn out and remove the lining paper. Serve cut into squares.

Plum and amaretti sponge cake slice

175g unsalted butter • 175g caster sugar • 3 large eggs • 175g self-raising flour, sifted • 2 tsp grated lemon zest • 1 tbsp fresh lemon juice • 3 plums, halved and stoned • 25g amaretti biscuits, coarsely crushed • 1 tbsp demerara sugar, for sprinkling

SERVES 6

Crushed amaretti add an interesting crunch to this tray-bake and the almond flavour works incredibly well with the plums. Serve with crème fraiche or vanilla ice cream.

1. Grease and line an 18 x 28cm baking tray with baking parchment. Preheat the oven to 180°C/350°F/gas 4.

2. Whisk the butter and sugar together until pale and fluffy (see page 28). Add the eggs a little at a time, beating well after each addition. Sift the flour over the top and fold in with the lemon zest and juice.

3. Spoon into the prepared tin and spread into the corners. Arrange the plums, skin side up, over the top then sprinkle with the amaretti and sugar. Bake until risen and golden, 45–50 minutes.

4. Remove from the tin and let the cake cool on a wire rack before removing the lining paper.

Classic cheesecake with blackberry topping

200g digestive biscuits, crushed • 65g butter, melted • 3 large eggs, separated •
175g caster sugar • 350g full fat soft cheese • 200ml soured cream • 2 tbsp cornflour •
2 tsp vanilla extract • 4 tsp grated lemon zest • For the topping • 450g blackberries •
100g caster sugar • 4 tsp arrowroot • 4 tbsp blackberry or cherry liqueur

SERVES 6–8

You can't beat a classic cheesecake when it comes to pleasing everyone. This baked lemon version is topped with a blackberry glaze but it is just as delicious with any soft berry fruit of your choice. Raspberry or blackcurrant are especially good.

1. Preheat the oven to 180°C/350°F/gas 4. Grease a 23cm springform tin and line the base with baking parchment. Mix the biscuits and butter together and press into the base of the tin.

2. Whisk the egg yolks and half the sugar until light and fluffy. Add the soft cheese a little at a time, whisking until smooth. Mix in the soured cream, cornflour, vanilla extract, lemon zest and the remaining sugar.

3. In a separate, non-reactive bowl beat the egg whites until stiff then fold them into the mixture. Pour into the tin and bake until just set and golden on top, 1–1¼ hours. Run a knife around the inside of the tin then let cool in the oven with the door open slightly.

4. Meanwhile, make the topping. Cook the blackberries in 4 tablespoons water until the juices run and the berries are soft, 5 minutes. Blend the arrowroot with the liqueur and stir into the fruit. Bring to a boil then remove from the heat and set aside to cool.

5. Remove the cheesecake from the tin. Pour the blackberries and glaze over the top of the cheesecake. Chill 4 hours before serving.

Curd cheese tarts

For the pastry • 100g plain flour • pinch salt • 65g chilled butter, cut into pieces • 2 tbsp caster sugar • ½ beaten egg • 1 tbsp cold water • For the filling • 250g curd cheese • 3 egg yolks • 2 tsp grated lemon zest • 1 tsp vanilla extract • 75g caster sugar • 4 tbsp double cream • icing sugar for dusting

MAKES 6 tarts

The filling for these little tartlets is enhanced with lemon zest. It's a kind of light cheesecake mixture cooked in individual pastry shells. Best served warm.

1. Put the flour, salt and butter in a food processor and pulse until the mixture looks like fine breadcrumbs. Add the sugar and pulse again to combine. Mix the egg and water together then pour into the machine and pulse the mixture until it forms a ball. Wrap in clear film and chill 30 minutes.

2. Preheat the oven to 200ºC/400ºF/gas 6. Use the pastry to line six deep brioche tins and trim off any excess. Line each with baking parchment and baking beans and bake blind, 15 minutes. Remove the paper and beans and return to the oven 5 minutes. Reduce the oven temperature to 170ºC/325ºF/gas 3.

3. Put the curd cheese, egg yolks, lemon zest, vanilla extract and sugar in a bowl and whisk together until smooth. Lightly whisk in the cream until smooth. Pour into the pastry cases. Bake until lightly set, 25–30 minutes. Let the tarts cool slightly then serve dusted with icing sugar.

angel food cake the basic method This classic

cake uses just the egg whites in the cake mixture and has no fat added whatsoever, which results in an extremely light and foamy sponge. It is cooked in a tube tin, left ungreased to encourage the mixture to cling to the sides as it rises. If it doesn't do this, you will have a cake which will sink dramatically when you take it out of the oven. To help it even further, the cake is cooled upside down in the tin to let it set.

step 1 Whisk the egg whites in a large bowl using a hand-held electric whisk, an egg whisk or a balloon whisk, until the whites are just foamy, before they become stiff.

step 2 Add cream of tartar and salt at this stage, then continue whisking the egg whites until they are stiff and form peaks when you lift up the beaters or whisk.

step 3 When the egg whites are at the stiff peak stage, gradually whisk in the sugar, a spoonful at a time, until the egg whites are both stiff and glossy.

step 4 Add the flour in three batches. Fold in each batch using a spatula or a large metal spoon, being careful not to knock out any air.

step 5 For the frosting, measure all the ingredients into a bowl, and put the bowl over a pan of hot water. Whisk with an electric hand-held whisk until thick.

Angel food cake

50g plain flour • 1 tbsp cornflour • 200g caster sugar • 7 egg whites • ¾ tsp cream of tartar • pinch of salt • 1 ½ tsp vanilla extract • For the frosting • 2 egg whites • 350g caster sugar • ¼ tsp cream of tartar • 2 tbsp toasted chopped pistachios, to decorate

SERVES 6–8

A truly magnificent feat of the art of cake-making, this cake seems to be held together purely by air!

1. Preheat the oven to 180°C/350°F/gas 4. Sift the flour and cornflour together. Add 75g of the sugar and sift together twice.

2. Whisk the egg whites until foamy. Add the cream of tartar and salt and continue whisking until stiff.

3. Whisk the remaining sugar into the egg whites until stiff and glossy. Whisk in the vanilla extract.

4. Fold in the flour then spoon into a 23cm springform tube tin. The mixture should come up to the top of the tin. Smooth over the top and bake until lightly golden on top and spongy to the touch, 45–50 minutes. Remove from the oven and invert onto a wire rack. Leave in the tin until cool.

5. For the frosting, put all the ingredients into a bowl, add 4 tablespoons water and put the bowl over a pan of hot water. Whisk with an electric hand-held whisk until thick, 10–12 minutes.

6. Run a knife round the sides of the tin and remove. Spread the frosting over the top. Finish with a sprinkle of pistachio nuts.

Strawberry ice cream angel cake

50g plain flour • 2 tbsp cornflour • 200g caster sugar • 7 large egg whites •
¾ tsp cream of tartar • pinch salt • 1 ½ tsp vanilla extract • For the filling •
4 tbsp strawberry jam • 500ml strawberry ice cream • fresh strawberries, to serve

SERVES 6–8

A deliciously light sponge cake filled with strawberry ice cream makes a dream dessert and looks a real picture. Remove from the freezer 30 minutes before serving and top with fresh strawberries for an extra-special touch.

1. Preheat the oven to 180°C/350°F/gas 4. Sift the flour and cornflour together. Add 75g caster sugar and sift together twice.

2. Whisk the egg whites in a non-reactive bowl until foamy. Add the cream of tartar and salt and continue whisking until they are stiff.

3. Whisk the remaining sugar into the egg whites a spoonful at a time until the egg whites form stiff peaks and are glossy. Whisk in the vanilla extract.

4. Fold in the flour in three batches then spoon into a 23cm springform tube tin. The mixture should come up to the top of the tin. Smooth over the top and bake until lightly golden on top and spongy to the touch, 45–50 minutes. Remove from the oven and invert onto a wire rack. Leave in the tin until cool.

5. Remove the cake from the tin and cool. Wash and dry the tin and line with baking parchment. Cut the cake horizontally and return the base to the pan. Spread the jam over the base and top with ice cream, spreading over evenly. Top with the other half and press down lightly. Freeze until firm. Serve topped with fresh strawberries.

Simple almond cake

250g ground almonds • 2 tbsp plain flour, sifted • 7 large egg whites •
200g caster sugar • 150ml double cream, whipped • 175g strawberries,
sliced • 2 tbsp orange liqueur • icing sugar for dusting

SERVES 6–8

**This light, moist cake is packed with ground almonds and
is delicious with fresh fruit and cream. Choose whichever
fruit you prefer and serve with fresh whipped cream for
added luxury.**

1. Preheat the oven to 180°C/350°F/gas 4. Grease and line a
23cm springform tin. Sift the almonds and flour together into a
bowl and set aside. Whisk the egg whites in a non-reactive bowl
until stiff. Keep whisking while gradually adding the sugar to form a
stiff meringue.

2. Gently fold in the flour and almond mixture. Spoon into the tin
and bake until golden and spongy to the touch, 25–30 minutes.

3. Cool in the tin then turn out and slice horizontally. Drizzle the
orange liqueur over each half. Spread one half with the whipped
cream and top with the sliced strawberries. Top with the second
half and dust with icing sugar before serving.

Cappuccino truffle cake

1 tbsp instant coffee powder • 150ml boiling water • 100g no-need-to-soak pitted prunes, chopped • 4 tbsp Tia Maria or other coffee liqueur • 175g 70% cocoa solid plain chocolate, broken into squares • 100g butter, plus extra for greasing • 5 eggs, separated • 100g caster sugar • 1 tsp vanilla extract • 1 tbsp cornflour • cocoa powder for dusting • whipped cream to serve

SERVES 6–8

This wickedly delicious coffee and chocolate cake is more like a cold soufflé than a cake. Enjoy with an espresso coffee at the end of a meal.

1. Dissolve the coffee powder in the boiling water, then pour over the prunes in a bowl with the Tia Maria. Let soak overnight.

2. Preheat the oven to 170°C/325°F/gas 3. Grease and line a deep 20cm springform tin with baking parchment.

3. Melt the chocolate and butter together in a bowl set over a pan of hot water. Whisk the egg yolks and caster sugar with an electric hand-held whisk until they until they reach the ribbon stage (see page 24). Stir in the vanilla extract, prune and melted chocolate mixtures and set aside.

4. With clean beaters, whisk the egg whites in a non-reactive bowl until stiff. Whisk in the cornflour and fold into the chocolate mixture. Pour into the prepared tin and bake until springy to the touch, 50 minutes. Allow to cool in the tin.

5. Cut into slices and serve topped with a spoonful of whipped cream and a dusting of cocoa powder.

meringues

meringues

A meringue mixture is made by whipping together just two ingredients, egg whites and sugar, until stiff and glossy. Meringues can be shaped before baking (usually at a low temperature for a long time, to ensure the mixture is fully dried out) and served with fruit, cream or other moist fillings. Some classic shapes are shown opposite. The mixture can also be heaped on top of a tangy fruit pie or incorporated into delectable cakes or macaroons.

meringue the basic method

When making a meringue mixture, the proportion of sugar should be 3 tablespoons to each egg white. A non-reactive copper bowl will produce the best foam with the greatest volume.

step 1 Whisk the egg whites to stiff peaks. Add half the sugar, 1 tablespoon at a time. Continue beating for 30 seconds. The meringue should be glossy and form short, soft peaks.

step 2 Fold in the rest of the sugar with a large metal spoon, carefully and thoroughly. The meringue should now be able to hold long stiff peaks when the whisk is lifted.

shaping meringues

quenelles Take two large metal spoons and scoop up some meringue with one of them. Scrape the meringue off onto the other spoon. Keep repeating until you have a smooth oval shape. Place on a lined baking sheet, and bake at 130ºC/250ºF/gas ½, for 3–4 hours.

fingers Fit a piping bag with a large plain piping nozzle. Spoon in the meringue and twist the top of the bag to seal. Pipe into fingers on a baking sheet lined with baking parchment. Bake at 130ºC/250ºF/gas ½, 3–4 hours.

nests Spoon the meringue into a piping bag fitted with a large star or plain nozzle and twist to seal the top of the bag. Pipe 10cm circles in spirals onto a lined baking tray. Pipe more meringue around the edges to make 'walls'. Bake at 130ºC/250ºF/gas ½, 1 hour.

Meringue nests

4 egg whites, at room temperature • 175g caster sugar • 1 tsp vanilla extract • whipped
double cream or crème fraiche • mixed berry fruits • icing sugar for dusting

SERVES 4

**Filled with fruit and cream, these are a delight. Or if you
are feeling particularly wicked, you could try ice cream
and fudge sauce with extra cream on top.**

1. Preheat the oven to 130°C/250°F/gas ½. Whisk the egg whites
to stiff peaks.

2. Gradually whisk in half the sugar, a spoonful at a time, then use
a metal spoon to fold in the remaining sugar. Fold in the vanilla
extract.

3. Pipe the meringue into nests (see page 51) on a baking tray
lined with baking parchment.

4. Bake 1 hour. Leave to cool on the trays. Fill with whipped cream
or crème fraiche, then top with mixed berry fruit and a dusting of
icing sugar.

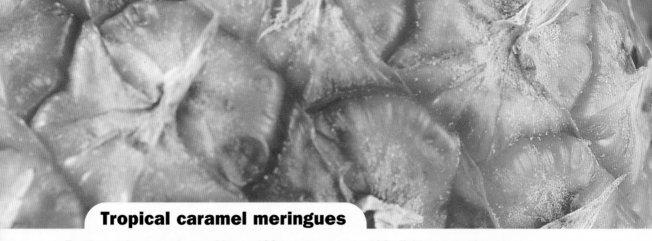

Tropical caramel meringues

For the meringues • **4 egg whites** • **100g caster sugar** • **100g light muscovado sugar** •
For the filling • **300g full fat soft cheese** • **175g icing sugar** • **3 canned pineapple rings,
drained well and finely chopped** • **2 tsp fresh lemon juice** • **2 peaches, stoned and sliced**

MAKES 14 single meringues

**Using muscovado sugar in the meringues gives them a
rich caramel flavour and fantastic golden colour. Here
they're filled with pineapple and peach slices, but coconut
ice cream and raspberry sauce taste good too.**

1. Preheat the oven to 130°C/250°F/gas ½. Whisk the egg whites
until stiff. Mix the two sugars together and then add to the egg
whites 1 tablespoon at a time, whisking well between each addition.

2. Line a baking sheet with baking parchment. Use two tablespoons
to shape the meringue into fourteen ovals (quenelles, see page 51).
Bake until thoroughly dried out, 3–4 hours.

3. Remove the meringues from the oven and let them cool on the
baking sheet.

4. To make the filling, beat the cheese to soften it then gradually
add the icing sugar, beating well between each addition. Stir in the
pineapple and lemon juice.

5. Spoon some filling onto half of the meringues, add a few slices of
peach and sandwich together with the remaining meringue halves.

Mixed berry basket

4 egg whites, at room temperature • 175g caster sugar • 1 tsp vanilla extract • **For the sauce** • 175g strawberries • 2 tbsp icing sugar • **For the filling** • 250g mascarpone cheese • 300ml double cream • 3 tbsp Cointreau or other orange liqueur • 350g mixed berry fruits, eg raspberries, blueberries, strawberries

SERVES 4

Use a plain meringue mixture to make a tray or basket and fill with any fruit of your choice. Here it is filled with a mixture of berries with a fragrant strawberry sauce drizzled over the top.

1. Line a baking sheet with baking parchment. Preheat the oven to 140°C/275°F/gas 1. Whisk the egg whites until stiff. Add the sugar a tablespoon at a time until it has nearly all been added.

2. Continue beating until glossy peaks form, 30 seconds. Use a metal spoon to fold in the remaining sugar then fold in the vanilla extract.

3. Spoon half the meringue onto the baking sheet and spread out to a 18 x 28cm rectangle. Either pipe a rope edge or small rosettes around the sides on top of the meringue base or drop small spoonfuls onto the edges to form a border. Bake 1 hour. Reduce the oven temperature to 130°C/250°F/gas ½ and continue cooking until the meringue is lightly coloured and crisp to the touch, 2–2½ hours. Let cool on the tray then run a palette knife underneath and transfer to a flat plate or board.

4. To make the sauce, purée the strawberries and icing sugar in a blender or food processor then sieve to remove the pips. Whip the mascarpone and cream together and stir in the Cointreau. Spoon into the meringue basket and top with the prepared fruits. Drizzle over some of the sauce to serve.

Raspberry and passion fruit pavlova

4 egg whites • 225g caster sugar • 1 tsp white wine vinegar • 1 ½ tsp cornflour •
1 tsp vanilla extract • For the topping • 600ml double cream • 350g fresh raspberries •
4 passion fruit • fresh mint sprigs • icing sugar for dusting

SERVES 4–6

This marshmallow-like meringue was created in Australia in the 1930s to celebrate the visit of the ballerina Anna Pavlova. It can be topped with any fruit you like but is particularly good if the fruit is a bit tart to complement the swee* meringue.

1. Preheat the oven to 180°C/350°F/gas 4. Line a baking tray with baking parchment. Whisk the egg whites until stiff. Whisk in the sugar 1 tablespoon at a time, whisking well between each addition.

2. Blend the vinegar, cornflour and vanilla extract together in a small bowl then whisk into the meringue mixture.

3. Spoon the mixture onto the paper-lined baking tray and spread out to a 25cm circle. Make a slight dip in the centre. Bake 5 minutes. Reduce the oven temperature to 150°C/300°F/gas 2, then bake until firm to the touch and lightly golden, 1¼ hours. Turn off the oven and let cool in the oven, 2–3 hours.

4. Slide a palette knife under the pavlova and transfer to a flat serving plate. Whip the cream until it forms soft peaks and spoon into the centre of the pavlova.

5. Scatter the raspberries over the top. Scoop the seeds and pulp out of the passion fruit and scatter onto the raspberries. Decorate with mint and dust with icing sugar.

Double chocolate mini alaskas

150g plain chocolate digestive biscuits, crushed · 40g butter, melted · 400ml good quality chocolate chip ice cream · 1 flaked chocolate bar, cut into four · 3 egg whites · 175g caster sugar · ½ tsp vanilla extract · cocoa powder for dusting

MAKES 4

These have a biscuit base for simplicity in place of the more usual cake base. Use the best quality ice cream you can find as it needs to freeze really firmly before being baked. Italian-style cooked meringue is more stable than the usual cold whipped method so it can withstand freezing and then high baking temperatures.

1. Mix the crushed biscuits with the melted butter. Place an 8cm round pastry cutter on a greased baking sheet and spoon a quarter of the crumbs into it. Press down well then remove the cutter. Repeat three times to make four bases.

2. Place the tray in a freezer to firm up, about 30 minutes. Soften the ice cream slightly then divide between the bases. Top each with a piece of flaked chocolate. Return to the freezer and leave until solid, 1–2 hours.

3. Whisk the egg whites, sugar and vanilla extract until frothy. Place the bowl over a pan of gently simmering water and continue whisking until the meringue is thick and glossy, about 10 minutes. Remove from the heat and continue whisking until cool.

4. Take the bases out of the freezer and cover each completely with the meringue. Return to the freezer and freeze at least 4 hours.

5. Preheat the oven to 220°C/425°F/gas 7. Bake until golden, 6–8 minutes. Dust with cocoa powder before serving.

Hazelnut meringue cake

4 egg whites · 225g caster sugar · 1 tsp vanilla extract · 1 tsp cider vinegar ·
1 tsp cornflour · 100g toasted hazelnuts, finely ground · 2 tbsp toasted, coarsely
chopped hazelnuts · For the filling · 200g plain yogurt · 2 tbsp bourbon · 2 tbsp clear
honey · 150ml double cream · 225g raspberries · icing sugar, for dusting

SERVES 6-8

**This rich and crumbly hazelnut meringue is filled with a
bourbon-laced cream and fresh raspberries and would
make a wonderfully impressive dessert to serve at a
dinner party. Fill about an hour before serving – any
longer and the meringue will start to soften.**

1. Preheat the oven to 180°C/350°F/gas 4. Grease and line the
bases of two 20cm round shallow cake tins with baking parchment.

2. Whisk the egg whites until stiff. Gradually whisk in the sugar until
it forms a stiff, glossy meringue. Fold in the vanilla extract, vinegar,
cornflour and ground hazelnuts.

3. Divide the mixture between the two tins and spread evenly.
Scatter the chopped hazelnuts over the top of one, then bake until
crisp, 50–60 minutes. Remove from the tins and leave to cool on a
wire rack.

4. While the meringues are cooling make the raspberry cream. Stir
the yogurt, bourbon and honey together, whip the cream until it
forms soft peaks then fold into the yogurt with the raspberries.
Sandwich the meringues together with the raspberry cream with the
nut-topped one on top. Dust with icing sugar before serving.

Lemon-lime meringue pie

350g shortcrust pastry • For the filling • grated zest and juice of 3 limes • grated zest and juice of 3 lemons • 150g caster sugar • 5 tbsp cornflour • 50g butter • 5 egg yolks • icing sugar for dusting • For the meringue • 5 egg whites • 275g caster sugar • ½ tsp vanilla extract • 1 tsp cider vinegar • 1 tsp cornflour

SERVES 6–8

Tangy, sweet and delicious, this deep pie will have them coming back for more. Good served chilled, too.

1. Roll out the pastry on a lightly floured surface and use to line a deep 23cm loose-bottomed fluted tin. Prick the base and chill 10 minutes. Preheat the oven to 200°C/400°F/gas 6. Line the pastry case with baking parchment and baking beans and bake blind, 15 minutes. Remove the paper and beans and return to the oven, 5 minutes. Reduce oven temperature to 150°C/300°F/gas 2.

2. For the filling, make up the lime and lemon juices in a measuring jug to 225ml with water if necessary. Pour into a saucepan with the zest and add 225ml water and the sugar. Heat gently to dissolve the sugar.

3. Mix the cornflour with 5 tablespoons cold water. Whisk the mixture into the juice. Continue whisking gently until thickened, then whisk in the butter and egg yolks. Bring to a boil over a low heat, whisking all the time, then simmer 3 minutes. Remove from the heat and set aside to cool slightly. Pour into the pastry case.

4. Whisk the egg whites until stiff. Gradually whisk in the sugar until glossy. Blend the vanilla extract, vinegar and cornflour together and fold into the meringue.

5. Place spoonfuls over the pie. Bake until lightly golden, 40–50 minutes. Allow to cool 20 minutes before serving.

Strawberry and pistachio vacherin

4 egg whites • 175g caster sugar • 50g light muscovado sugar • 50g toasted finely
chopped pistachio nuts • For the filling • 300ml double cream • 2 tbsp icing sugar •
2 tbsp coconut rum • To decorate • 225g strawberries • fresh mint leaves

SERVES 4

**A vacherin is a cold meringue dessert, named after the
wheel of cheese it resembles. Finely chopped pistachios
flavour this meringue mixture and also give it a lovely
chewy, nutty centre. Make sure the meringue is really
thick and glossy before folding in the nuts.**

1. Preheat the oven to 140°C/275°F/gas 1 . Line two baking
sheets with baking parchment and draw a 20cm circle on each
sheet. Turn them over so the pencil marks are on the underside.

2. Whisk the egg whites until stiff. Mix the sugars together then
add to the egg whites a spoonful at a time until all the sugar has
been added. Fold in the nuts.

3. Spoon the meringue into a piping bag fitted with a plain nozzle.
Pipe the meringue in a spiral starting from the centre of each circle
to make two circles. Bake until crisp to the touch and lightly
coloured, 1–1$^{1}/_{2}$ hours. Let cool in the turned-off oven then
carefully peel off the paper.

4. Make the filling by whipping the cream, icing sugar and coconut
rum together until it forms soft peaks. Spread three-quarters of the
cream over one meringue circle. Top with some sliced strawberries
and then the other meringue.

5. Top with spoonfuls of the cream and finish with halved
strawberries and mint leaves.

Chocolate and chestnut macaroon cake

300g icing sugar • ½ tsp bicarbonate of soda • 4 large egg whites • 175g ground almonds • For the filling • 100g chestnut purée • 2 tbsp maple syrup • 75g plain chocolate • 250g mascarpone cheese • 150ml double cream • chocolate curls, to decorate

SERVES 6–8

This three-layered almond meringue cake is filled with a rich chestnut and chocolate-flavoured cream. To give it an extra-special finish each serving can be drizzled thinly with melted dark chocolate.

1. Line three baking sheets with baking parchment and draw an 18cm circle on each. Preheat the oven to 140°C/275°F/gas 1. Sift the icing sugar and bicarbonate of soda together.

2. Whisk the egg whites until stiff. Gradually beat in three-quarters of the icing sugar until the mixture is stiff and glossy. Mix the rest into the ground almonds and fold into the whites. Divide the mixture between the three circles and spread out evenly. Bake 10 minutes. Reduce the oven temperature to 130°C/250°F/gas ½ and cook an additional 1¼ hours. Cool on a wire rack then peel away the paper.

3. Beat the chestnut purée and maple syrup together until smooth. Melt the chocolate in a bowl set over a pan of hot water. Stir the melted chocolate into the chestnut purée then beat in the mascarpone followed by the cream.

4. Place a meringue circle on a plate and spread with half of the chestnut mixture. Place a second meringue on top and spread that with the remaining chestnut mixture. Top with the remaining meringue round. Decorate the top with chocolate curls.

Almond macaroons

100g ground almonds • 175g caster sugar • 2 tbsp semolina or ground rice • 2 egg whites • a few drops of almond extract • 100g plain chocolate chips • whole blanched almonds, to decorate

MAKES 12 macaroons

Macaroons are traditionally made on edible rice paper, but if you have trouble finding it, then dust the baking sheets liberally with semolina and flour.

1. Preheat the oven to 170ºC/325ºF/gas 3. Line two baking sheets with rice paper.

2. Mix the almonds, sugar and semolina. In a separate bowl, whisk the egg whites until stiff. Add the almond extract.

3. Gradually fold in the sugar and almond mixture until quite stiff.

4. Fold in the chocolate chips. Place tablespoonsful of mixture onto the baking sheets, spaced out. Place an almond on top of each and bake until golden, 15–20 minutes. Cool, then tear the rice paper between each biscuit, or use a wire rack if you're not using paper.

Blueberry and white chocolate meringue roll

275g caster sugar • ½ vanilla pod • 5 egg whites • icing sugar for dusting • For the filling • 150g white chocolate • 250g mascarpone cheese • 100ml plain yogurt • 100g blueberries

SERVES 6

This is rather an unusual idea, using a meringue mixture to roll into a roulade-type dessert. The filling is a white chocolate cream with tangy, fragrant blueberries throughout.

1. Preheat the oven to 220°C/425°F/gas 7. Grease and line a 23 x 33cm Swiss roll tin with waxed paper.

2. Combine the sugar and the seeds from inside the vanilla pod. Whisk the egg whites until stiff. Gradually whisk in the vanilla sugar a spoonful at a time until it forms a stiff, glossy meringue.

3. Spread the meringue mixture into the prepared tin and bake 8 minutes. Lower the oven temperature to 170°C/325°F/gas 3 and continue cooking until firm to the touch, 10 minutes.

4. Remove the meringue from the oven and turn out onto a sheet of baking parchment dusted with icing sugar. Peel off the lining paper from the base and let cool 10 minutes.

5. Meanwhile, make the filling. Melt the chocolate in a bowl set over hot water. Stir in the yogurt then beat into the mascarpone. Spread the cream over the meringue and top with the blueberries. Roll up from one of the long sides using the paper underneath to help. Leave wrapped in the paper at least 1 hour before serving.

ice creams and
other desserts

ice creams and other desserts

Smooth, creamy ice cream is everyone's favourite comfort food. It's easier to make than you think – you don't even need a specialist ice cream maker – and the possibilities for different and delicious flavourings are endless. This chapter also features a selection of miscellaneous desserts that use whipping techniques – trifles, sorbets, mousses and that sublime Italian creation, zabaglione.

ice cream the basic method

An ice cream base is made by combining a custard mixture with whipped cream. It's frozen for short bursts and whisked to break down the ice crystals formed during freezing.

step 1 Remove the vanilla pod from the heated milk. Whisk the egg yolks and sugar with a hand-held electric whisk until pale and slightly thickened. Lightly whisk in the hot milk.

step 2 Pour into a heavy-based pan. Cook over low heat, stirring constantly until the mixture thickens to the consistency of double cream and coats the back of the spoon.

step 3 Tear off some clear film and then press down gently over the surface of the custard (this will stop a skin from forming) and set to one side to go cold.

step 4 Pour the cream into a bowl. Using a hand-held electric whisk, whip the cream until it forms stiff peaks. When the custard is cold, fold in the cream.

step 5 Pour into a freezer container and freeze until half-frozen. Whisk to break up the ice crystals then return to the freezer. Repeat twice more until thick. Stir in flavourings and, finally, freeze until firm. Alternatively, churn in an ice cream maker.

Blue Lagoon ice cream

150ml full fat milk • ½ vanilla pod • 2 egg yolks • 5 tbsp caster sugar •
225g blueberries • 1 tbsp white rum • 300ml double cream • 40g meringues,
coarsely crushed

SERVES 6

**If you want to make plain vanilla ice cream, omit the
blueberry sauce and meringues and freeze. Or, if you
want to use any other fruit or chocolate sauce, swirl
them in, as for the blueberries, at the end.**

1. Bring the milk and vanilla pod to simmering point over low heat.
Remove the pan from the heat then remove the vanilla pod. Whisk
the egg yolks and 4 tablespoons of the sugar with an electric hand-
held whisk until pale and slightly thickened, then whisk in the milk.

2. Return to a clean, heavy-based, non-stick saucepan. Cook over
a low heat, stirring continuously until the mixture thickens. Cover
with clear film and let cool. Meanwhile, cook the blueberries with
the remaining sugar and 1 tablespoon water until broken up, 2
minutes. Cool then stir in the rum.

3. Whip the cream and fold into the custard. Pour into a shallow
freezerproof container and freeze until half-frozen, about 2–3 hours.
then beat with an electric hand-held mixer. Repeat this process at
least twice more until thick. Alternatively, churn in an ice cream
maker.

4. Swirl the meringues through the ice cream followed quickly by
the blueberry sauce, to make a marbled appearance. Spoon into a
freezerproof container and freeze until firm. Remove from the
freezer 20–30 minutes before serving.

Coffee and maple ice cream

150ml full fat milk • ½ vanilla pod • 2 egg yolks • 2 tbsp caster sugar • 2 tbsp instant coffee • 3 tbsp maple syrup • 300ml double cream • 2 tbsp coarsely chopped pecan nuts

SERVES 6

This ice cream is flavoured with an unbeatable combination of coffee and maple syrup and has pieces of pecan stirred through to give an irresistible crunch.

1. Heat the milk and vanilla pod together over a low heat until the milk almost boils. Remove from the heat and remove the vanilla pod. Whisk the egg yolks and sugar together until pale and slightly thickened, then whisk in the milk.

2. Return the mixture to a heavy-based non-stick saucepan. Cook over a low heat, stirring continuously until the mixture thickens to the consistency of double cream. Stir in the coffee granules and maple syrup until the coffee granules have dissolved. Cover the surface of the mixture with clear film and let cool.

3. Whip the cream until it forms soft peaks. Fold into the custard. Pour into a freezerproof container, place in the freezer until half-frozen, about 2–3 hours, and whisk to break up the ice crystals. Repeat twice more. Alternatively, churn in an ice cream maker.

4. When almost fully frozen, swirl in the pecans. Spoon into a freezerproof container and freeze until firm. Remove from the freezer 20–30 minutes before serving.

Blackcurrant and white rum fool

450g fresh or frozen blackcurrants · 50g caster sugar · 2 tbsp fresh orange juice ·
2 tbsp white rum · 300ml double cream, lightly whipped · For the custard · 150ml full
fat milk · ½ vanilla pod · 2 egg yolks · 50g caster sugar

SERVES 4

A fool is a combination of puréed fruit, custard and whipped cream and, in fact, it's not unlike an unfrozen ice cream mixture. Tart fruit seem to work best, so use fruits such as rhubarb, gooseberries, plums or, as here, blackcurrants.

1. Make a fruit purée by cooking the blackcurrants, caster sugar and orange juice in a covered pan until very soft, 5 minutes. Let cool then purée in a food processor or blender. Push the juice and pulp through a sieve. Stir in the white rum and set aside.

2. For the custard, heat the milk and vanilla pod together over a low heat until the milk almost boils. Remove from the heat and remove the vanilla pod. Whisk the egg yolks and sugar together until pale and slightly thickened, then whisk in the milk.

3. Return the mixture to a heavy-based non-stick saucepan. Cook over a low heat, stirring continuously, until the mixture thickens to the consistency of double cream. Cover the surface with clear film and let cool.

4. Stir the blackcurrant purée into the custard and then gently fold in the whipped cream. Stir gently until it thickens slightly then spoon into glasses and chill before serving.

Candied fruit bombe

4 tbsp dark rum or brandy · 150g mixed dried fruit, eg apricots, raisins, figs, cherries and cranberries, chopped · 300ml full fat milk · 1 vanilla pod · 2 egg yolks · 50g caster sugar · 300ml double cream · 50g plain chocolate, grated · fresh figs and mint sprigs to serve

SERVES 6

You can make this weeks ahead, so it's really great for entertaining. If you want to make it even easier on yourself, use a good quality ready-made custard instead of the egg custard in the recipe.

1. Pour the rum or brandy over the fruit and soak overnight. The next day, heat the milk and vanilla pod to simmering point over low heat. Remove from the heat. Whisk the egg yolks and sugar with an electric hand-held mixer until pale and slightly thickened, then whisk in the hot milk.

2. Return to a clean, heavy-based non-stick saucepan. Cook over a low heat, stirring continuously with a wooden spoon until the mixture thickens to the consistency of double cream. Cover the surface of the mixture with clear film and set aside to cool. Remove the vanilla pod.

3. Lightly whip the cream until it forms soft peaks then fold into the custard. Freeze in a shallow freezerproof container until half-frozen, about 2–3 hours, then whisk and return to the freezer. Repeat this process at least twice more until it holds its shape. Alternatively, churn in an ice cream maker. Mix in the rum-soaked fruits and the chocolate.

4. Spoon into a clear film-lined 900g pudding basin or six individual pudding basins. Freeze until firm. Remove from the freezer 30 minutes before serving. Turn out and remove the clear film. Serve with fresh figs and mint sprigs.

Caribbean coconut trifle

350g sweet pineapple flesh • 300ml double cream •
4 tbsp coconut milk • 200ml crème fraîche • 4 tbsp icing sugar •
2 papaya, peeled, seeded and chopped • 2 mangoes, peeled,
stoned and chopped • juice of 1 lime • toasted flaked coconut,
to decorate

SERVES 6

**This trifle is actually based on a Caribbean fruit fool –
fruit stirred into thick vanilla-flavoured cream.**

1. Cut the pineapple into large chunks, put in a food processor or
blender and process briefly until chopped. Tip into a sieve and let
the juice drain away, or reserve to drink later.

2. Whip the cream until it forms soft peaks, then lightly fold in the
coconut milk, crème fraîche and icing sugar.

3. Fold the drained pineapple into the cream mixture. Put the
papaya and mango in a large serving bowl and pour over the lime
juice and 4 tablespoons of the drained pineapple juice.

4. Spoon the pineapple cream on top of the fruit and scatter over
the toasted coconut flakes.

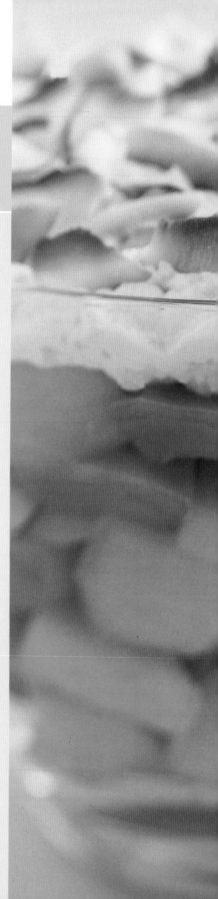

right: **Caribbean coconut trifle**

Kahlua and chocolate trifle

150ml strong fresh coffee • 4 tbsp Kahlua or other coffee liqueur • 175g bought or home-made sponge fingers (see page 20) • 75g caster sugar • 2 tsp vanilla extract • 500g mascarpone cheese • 300ml double cream • 100g plain chocolate, grated • cocoa powder, to serve

SERVES 4–6

This is based on the Italian tiramisu, which is traditionally flavoured with coffee and laced with liqueur. Kahlua gives the fresh coffee a bit of a kick.

1. Grease and line a 900g loaf tin with clear film. Mix the coffee and Kahlua together. Dip the sponge fingers into the mixture and use some to line the base of the tin.

2. Whisk the sugar and vanilla extract into the mascarpone. Add the cream a little at a time, whisking on a slow speed until smooth.

3. Spoon half of the mixture on top of the sponge fingers in the tin and spread over evenly. Add half the grated chocolate then repeat a layer of the dipped sponge fingers, the remaining creamed mixture, grated chocolate and a final layer of dipped sponge fingers. Drizzle any remaining coffee mixture over the top.

4. Cover with a layer of clear film then chill, 2–3 hours. Remove from the tin and peel off the clear film. Dust with a generous amount of cocoa powder, slice and serve.

Lychee sorbet

6 tbsp caster sugar • 425g can lychees in syrup • 1 tbsp elderflower cordial •
1 egg white

SERVES 6

**Elderflower cordial adds a wonderful,
scented flavour to this simple, refreshing
sorbet, but if it's hard to find, lemonade
will have a similar effect. Whipped egg
whites are added to lighten.**

1. Heat the sugar and 250ml water together until
the sugar has dissolved. Bring to the boil and
simmer 1 minute. Remove from the heat and
allow to cool.

2. Purée the lychees and syrup in a food
processor or blender then pass through a sieve,
pressing down well to extract all the juice. Add the
elderflower cordial.

3. Pour the mixture into a shallow freezerproof
container and freeze until just beginning to hold
its shape, about 2–3 hours.

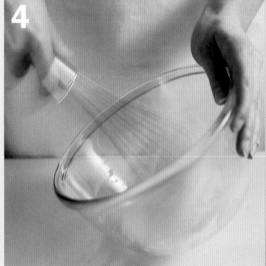

4. Whisk the egg white until it forms soft peaks
then add to the sorbet. Continue freezing and
whisking by hand until it becomes thick and
creamy. Freeze until required.

5. Remove from the freezer and put in the
refrigerator 5–10 minutes before serving.

Chilled mandarin and lemon mousse

grated zest and juice of 1 lemon • grated zest of 2 mandarins and the juice of 4 mandarins • 1 sachet powdered gelatine • 4 eggs, separated • 100g caster sugar • 300ml double cream • whipped cream, to decorate • pared lemon and mandarin zest, to decorate

MAKES 6 SMALL GLASSES

This fresh, fruity summer dessert looks so pretty decorated with little twists of lemon and mandarin peel.

1. Put the fruit zest in a bowl. Measure the fruit juice - it should be no more than 250ml. Pour the measured juice into a small saucepan and sprinkle the gelatine in. Let soak for 5 minutes, then heat gently without boiling until the gelatine has dissolved. Let cool.

2. Add the egg yolks and sugar to the fruit zest and whisk until the mixture is very thick and creamy.

3. With clean beaters, whisk the egg whites until stiff and whip the cream until it forms soft peaks. Gently whisk the gelatine mixture into the yolks, then fold in the cream and finally the egg whites.

4. Spoon the mixture into glasses and chill until set, 3–4 hours. Decorate with whipped cream and lemon and mandarin peel.

Note: Recipes using raw eggs should be avoided by infants, the elderly, pregnant women and anyone with a compromised immune system.

Rich mocha pots

175g plain chocolate, broken into pieces • 3 tbsp strong black coffee • 15g butter •
4 eggs, separated • 2 tbsp brandy • 4 tbsp icing sugar • whipped cream, to decorate •
grated chocolate or curls, to decorate

MAKES 6–8 pots

This dark, sultry take on chocolate mousse is a sophisticated, grown-up dessert. For best results use the finest chocolate you can find and chill the mousse well before serving.

1. Melt the chocolate in a bowl set over a pan of hot water. Stir in the coffee and butter until smooth. Remove from the heat and whisk in the egg yolks one by one until the mixture is smooth and glossy. Whisk in the brandy then set aside to cool and thicken slightly while you are whisking the egg whites.

2. Whisk the egg whites in a non-reactive bowl until stiff. Gradually add the sugar and continue whisking until glossy and thick. Fold into the cooled chocolate mixture.

3. Pour into six or eight small teacups or professional ramekins and chill until firm, 3–4 hours. Top with whipped cream and the grated chocolate or chocolate curls.

Note: Recipes using raw eggs should be avoided by infants, the elderly, pregnant women and anyone with a compromised immune system.

Creamy zabaglione

4 egg yolks • 4 tbsp caster sugar • 100ml Marsala • grated zest of ½ lemon •
150ml double cream, whipped • ½ tsp vanilla extract • sponge fingers or
biscotti to serve

SERVES 4

**Whisking over hot water heats up the mixture and lets
the egg yolks cook and thicken the mixture. Take care
though – if it overheats, it will separate.**

1. Put the egg yolks and sugar into a bowl and whisk over
simmering water with an electric hand-held whisk until the mixture
is pale yellow, creamy and smooth.

2. Add the Marsala a little at a time, whisking constantly until the
mixture is very light and almost thick enough to leave a trail when
the beaters are lifted.

3. Remove the bowl from the heat and whisk an additional 5
minutes. Fold in the lemon zest, whipped cream and vanilla extract
and serve in glasses with sponge fingers or biscotti to dip in.

Seared fruit in frothy orange sauce

2 fresh figs • ½ sweet pineapple, peeled and cored • 1 ripe mango • 175g blackberries • 4 tbsp white wine • 75g caster sugar • 6 egg yolks • 2 tbsp Cointreau or other orange liqueur

SERVES 4

This out-of-the-ordinary gratin is strictly for adults. A colourful combination of tropical fruits are covered with a frothy, egg-based sauce flavoured with orange liqueur.

1. Cut the figs into wedges and the pineapple into chunks. Peel the mango, cut the flesh off the stone and then cut into chunky pieces.

2. Divide the prepared fruit between four individual gratin dishes and scatter the blackberries over the top.

3. Heat the wine and sugar in a saucepan until the sugar has dissolved. Cook 4–5 minutes.

4. Put the egg yolks in a large heatproof bowl. Place over a pan of simmering water and whisk the yolks until they are pale, thick and fluffy. Slowly pour the syrup into the egg yolks, with the Cointreau, whisking all the time until it thickens.

5. Spoon the frothy mixture over the fruit and place under a hot grill on a low shelf until the topping is golden. Serve immediately.

Cherry syllabub

100ml sweet white wine • 50ml white or coconut rum • 2 tbsp fresh lemon juice • 90g caster sugar • 425ml double cream • 300g fresh pitted cherries • crisp almond biscuits, to serve

SERVES 4

The joy of this dessert is that any flavoured liqueur or spirit of your choice can be added to the basic mixture. Also the fruit can be varied depending on the season and your preference.

1. In a large bowl combine the white wine, rum, lemon juice and sugar, and mix well until the sugar has dissolved.

2. Stir in the cream and then whip until stiff enough to hold soft peaks. Spoon the cherries into the bases of four glasses and top with the cream syllabub.

3. Serve immediately with crisp almond biscuits to dip into the cream. If left to stand for too long the mixture will separate out again.

soufflés

soufflés

Soufflé is a French word which literally means 'puffed up'. In cooking it's used to describe a light, frothy dish, just stiff enough to hold its shape. Whether sweet or savoury, soufflés should be firm on the outside and deliciously wobbly in the centre. This chapter also includes roulades – sophisticated-looking, rolled-up variations on the classic soufflé – and soufflé omelettes, which are so much lighter and fluffier than standard omelettes.

soufflés the basic method

The classic soufflé is made by mixing a thick, flavoured sauce, with flour and butter as its base, with whisked egg whites, which expand in the oven to give the soufflé its puffy appearance.

step 1 Melt the butter in a large saucepan, add the flour and cook 1 minute. Remove from the heat and whisk in the milk. Bring to the boil, stirring, until the sauce has thickened.

step 2 Remove from the heat and add flavourings. Let the mixture cool for a few minutes. Whisk in the egg yolks one at a time until the sauce is smooth and glossy.

step 3 With clean beaters and in a separate bowl, whisk the egg whites until stiff but not dry. This is just before they reach the stiff peak stage.

step 4 Take a large spoonful of the whisked egg whites and beat it into the flavoured sauce base to slacken it a bit. Then, gently fold in the rest of the whisked egg whites.

step 5 Pour the mixture into a soufflé dish. Run your finger around the top inside edge of the dish. When the soufflé is baked, this is what gives it its 'top hat' appearance.

Cheese soufflé

50g butter, plus extra for greasing • 50g plain flour • 300ml milk • 5 eggs, separated • pinch of freshly grated nutmeg • ¼ tsp English mustard powder • 225g Cheddar, grated • 1 tbsp freshly grated Parmesan

SERVES 4

After mixing, the soufflé mixture can be kept in a refrigerator for an hour or two but should be served immediately after baking as the dramatic rise won't last for ever. This cheese soufflé has a crisp Parmesan crust and a delicious soft centre.

1. Preheat the oven to 180°C/350°F/gas 4. Grease a 1.5 litre soufflé dish with butter. Melt the remaining butter in a large saucepan, add the flour and cook 1 minute. Whisk in the milk then bring to the boil, stirring until thickened. Remove from the heat and add the nutmeg, mustard and seasoning. Stir in the Cheddar and allow to cool a few minutes.

2. Whisk in the egg yolks. Whisk the egg whites until stiff but not dry, beat in 1 tablespoon then fold in the rest.

3. Pour the mixture into the soufflé dish and run your finger around the top inside edge. Sprinkle with Parmesan and bake, 30–40 minutes.

Apple and Calvados soufflé

40g butter, plus extra for greasing · 15g digestive biscuit crumbs · 40g plain flour · 175ml milk · 3 tbsp Calvados or other apple brandy · 2 cooking apples, peeled, cored and sliced · 2 tsp grated lemon zest · 2 tbsp fresh lemon juice · 100g caster sugar · 4 eggs, separated · icing sugar for dusting

SERVES 4

A deliciously boozy dessert, this fantastic soufflé combines tart apples with sweet Calvados. Individual dishes look the most impressive but if you don't have them, one large dish will do.

1. Grease six 300ml soufflé dishes or a 1.7 litre soufflé dish with butter and scatter the biscuit crumbs around the sides and over the base. Preheat the oven to 190ºC/375ºF/gas 5.

2. Melt the remaining butter in a saucepan and add the flour. Remove from the heat and gradually stir in the milk. Return the pan to the heat and bring to the boil, stirring, until it thickens.

3. Cook 1 minute then remove from the heat and whisk in the Calvados. Cover the sauce with clear film. Set aside to cool.

4. Cook the apples with the lemon zest and juice and 1 tablespoon sugar in a covered pan, stirring occasionally until they form a purée, 5–6 minutes. Let cool slightly. Meanwhile whisk the egg yolks into the sauce then stir in the apple purée.

5. Whisk the egg whites until stiff. Gradually whisk in the remaining sugar until the meringue is glossy. Stir a spoonful of the egg whites into the sauce then fold in the rest. Spoon into dishes, run a finger around the edge and bake, 20–35 minutes, depending on dish size. Dust the top with icing sugar before serving.

Mushroom and garlic soufflé

For the sauce • 20g butter, plus extra for greasing • 20g plain flour • 250ml milk • pinch grated nutmeg • 50g mild goats' cheese • 4 eggs, separated • For the flavouring • 15g butter • 300g chestnut or field mushrooms, halved and finely sliced • 2 garlic cloves, crushed • 2 tbsp freshly chopped parsley • 1 tsp fresh thyme leaves

SERVES 4

Use mushrooms with a good strong flavour and a low water content such as chestnut or field mushrooms as they will give the best result. This recipe would be ideal to serve as a starter served with a mixed green salad.

1. Preheat the oven to 190°C/375°F/gas 5. Grease a 1.5 litre soufflé dish with butter. Melt the remaining butter in a large saucepan, add the flour and cook 1 minute. Remove from the heat, whisk in the milk then bring to the boil, stirring, until the sauce has thickened. Remove from the heat and add the nutmeg and seasoning. Stir in the cheese and let cool a few minutes.

2. For the flavouring, melt the butter in a large frying pan and cook the mushrooms over a medium heat until softened and all the liquid has evaporated. Stir in the garlic, cook 1 minute then leave to cool.

3. Whisk the egg yolks into the sauce, one at a time, until well incorporated and the sauce is smooth and glossy. Stir in the mushrooms and herbs.

4. With a clean whisk, whisk the egg whites until stiff. Stir a large spoonful of the egg whites into the sauce to slacken it a bit, then gently fold in the rest.

5. Pour the mixture into the soufflé dish. Run your finger around the edge and bake, 30–35 minutes.

Sweet vanilla soufflé

300ml milk • 1 vanilla pod, split • 100g caster sugar • 50g butter • 50g plain flour •
3 large eggs, separated • 1 egg white • icing sugar, for dusting

SERVES 6

This light and airy dessert makes a delicious end to any special meal.

1. Bring the milk, vanilla pod and sugar to the boil over a low heat, then set aside to cool.

2. Scrape the vanilla seeds out of the pod with the point of a sharp knife, and add to the milk. Discard the pod. Melt the butter in a small saucepan and stir in the flour. Cook 1 minute. Remove from the heat and gradually whisk in the milk. Return the pan to the heat and bring to the boil, stirring all the time.

3. Cook 1 minute then remove from the heat and cover the surface of the sauce with clear film. Set aside to cool slightly.

4. Preheat the oven to 190°C/375°F/gas 5. Liberally butter six 175ml soufflé dishes and dust the insides with sugar. Whisk the egg yolks into the cooled sauce until smooth. Whisk the egg whites until stiff. Spoon half into the sauce and stir in gently. Fold in the remaining egg whites with a metal spoon.

5. Pour into the dishes. Bake until well risen and lightly set, 20–25 minutes. Dust the tops with icing sugar before serving.

Spinach roulade

175g fresh spinach • 40g plain flour, plus extra for dusting • 40g butter, plus extra for greasing • 450ml milk • ¼ tsp grated nutmeg • 3 medium eggs, separated • 4 tbsp freshly grated Parmesan cheese • 200g garlic and herb full fat soft cheese • 75g ricotta • 2 tbsp sour cream • 2 tbsp fresh snipped chives

SERVES 6 as a starter or 4 as a main course

Another delicious presentation of a soufflé, this time as a soft, puffy roulade.

1. Preheat the oven to 200°C/400°F/gas 6. Wash the spinach and cook in a covered saucepan until just wilted, 2–3 minutes. Cool slightly, squeeze out all the moisture and finely chop. Grease and line a 23 x 33cm Swiss roll tin with waxed paper. Grease the paper and dust lightly with flour.

2. Melt the butter in a saucepan and stir in the flour. Cook 1 minute then remove from the heat. Gradually whisk in the milk then return to the heat and continue whisking gently until the mixture boils and thickens. Boil 1 minute then remove from the heat.

3. Whisk in the egg yolks one at a time until the mixture is smooth. Beat in the spinach, seasoning and nutmeg.

4. Whisk the egg whites until stiff and fold into the mixture. Pour the mixture into the tin and spread over evenly. Bake until lightly set, 12–14 minutes.

5. Sprinkle the Parmesan over a sheet of baking parchment and turn the roulade out onto it. Peel off the lining paper and allow to cool slightly. Beat the garlic and herb cheese, ricotta, soured cream and chives together. Spread over the roulade then use the paper to roll it up from one long side. Serve sliced with a mixed green salad.

Festive chocolate and hazelnut roulade

175g plain chocolate • 6 eggs, separated • 175g caster sugar • 75g ground hazelnuts • icing sugar, for dredging • **For the whipped cream** • 300ml double cream • 1 tbsp brandy

SERVES 6-8

This special dessert is really easy to make – start in the morning before the meal or even the day before. If serving at Christmas decorate with chocolate holly leaves before dusting with extra icing sugar.

1. Preheat the oven to 180°C/350°F/gas 4. Grease and line a 23 x 33 cm Swiss roll tin with baking parchment. Melt the chocolate in a bowl set over hot water, then set aside to cool slightly.

2. Whisk the egg yolks and sugar until the mixture is thick, smooth and glossy. In a separate bowl with a clean whisk, whisk the egg whites until stiff.

3. Fold the cooled chocolate and the ground hazelnuts into the egg yolk mixture. Gently stir in half the egg whites, then fold in the rest. Pour the mixture into the prepared tin then bake until risen and firm to the touch, 20 minutes. Cool in the tin, covered with a cooling rack and clean damp tea towel.

4. Whip the cream and brandy together until it forms soft peaks. Liberally dredge a piece of baking parchment with icing sugar, then turn the roulade out onto it. Peel off the lining paper and spread over the cream.

5. Use the paper to help you roll the roulade from one of the long sides. Transfer to a plate while still wrapped in the rolling paper. Remove the paper and sift extra sugar over it if needed. Cut into slices and serve with extra whipped cream if desired.

Cherry and berry roulade

5 large eggs, separated · 150g caster sugar · 75g creamed coconut, grated · icing sugar, for dredging · 2 tbsp flaked coconut · For the filling ·225g mixed frozen summer fruits with cherries · 1 tbsp fresh orange juice · 2 tsp cornflour · 2 tsp kirsch · 150ml double cream

SERVES 6–8

This featherlight sponge cake encloses a sumptuous selection of tangy berries and a decadent kirsch-flavoured whipped cream.

1. Preheat the oven to 180°C/350°F/gas 4. Grease and line a 23 x 33cm Swiss roll tin with baking parchment. Whisk the egg yolks and sugar until the mixture is thick, smooth and glossy. In a separate bowl, whisk the egg whites until stiff.

2. Fold the coconut into the egg yolk mixture. Gently stir in half the egg whites, then fold in the rest. Pour the mixture into the prepared tin then bake until risen and firm to the touch, 20 minutes. Cool in the tin, covered with a cooling rack and a clean, damp tea towel.

3. Cook the fruit in a saucepan with the orange juice until the juices begin to run. Blend the cornflour with a little water and stir into the fruit. Cook until thickened then remove from the heat and set aside to cool. Whip the cream and kirsch together until it forms soft peaks. Liberally dredge a piece of waxed paper with icing sugar, then turn the roulade out onto it. Peel off the lining paper and spread over the whipped cream and then spoon on the fruit.

4. Use the paper underneath to help you roll the roulade from one of the long sides so that it doesn't crack. Transfer to a plate while still wrapped in the rolling paper. Top with flaked coconut and sift extra icing sugar on top if needed. Cut into slices and serve with extra whipped cream as desired.

Apricot and almond omelette

2 eggs, separated · 25g caster sugar, plus extra to serve · butter, for frying ·
2 tbsp apricot jam · 1 tbsp fresh orange juice · 4 canned apricot halves, sliced ·
1 tbsp toasted flaked almonds

SERVES 2

**Whisked egg whites folded into a basic omelette mixture
make a wonderfully light, puffy soufflé omelette that can
be served with all sorts of fillings.**

1. Whisk the egg yolks and sugar in a bowl until thick.

2. In another bowl, with clean beaters, whisk the whites until they
form stiff peaks. Fold the egg whites into the egg yolk mixture.

3. Melt the butter in a small frying pan. Add the omelette mixture,
and cook until well risen and golden underneath, 2–3 minutes.
Place the frying pan under a hot grill 1 minute to set.

4. Melt the jam with the orange juice, boil for 1 minute then stir in
the sliced apricots. Spoon over the top of the omelette and fold over
quickly. Tip onto a plate and scatter with the flaked almonds. Dust
with caster sugar before serving.

Butterscotch and banana soufflé omelette

For the sauce • 20g butter • 40g light muscovado sugar • 1 tbsp golden syrup •
50ml double cream • 2 tbsp pecan nuts, broken into pieces • For the omelette •
2 eggs, separated • 25g caster sugar, plus extra for dusting • 15g butter • To serve •
vanilla ice cream • 1 banana, sliced

SERVES 1–2

**This light and fluffy sweet omelette is topped with sliced
bananas, vanilla ice cream and a special pecan and
butterscotch sauce – a great combination of hot and cold.**

1. First make the sauce. Melt the butter, sugar and syrup together
in a small saucepan. Stir in the cream and nuts and bring to the
boil. Remove from the heat and set aside.

2. For the omelette, put the egg yolks in a bowl with the sugar and
whisk until the mixture is thick and creamy.

3. In another bowl, with clean beaters, whisk the egg whites until
stiff. Fold into the egg yolk mixture until evenly incorporated.

4. Melt the butter in a small frying pan and add the omelette
mixture, spreading over the base with a palette knife. Cook until
well risen and golden underneath, 2–3 minutes. Place the frying
pan under a hot grill until pale golden on top, 1 minute.

5. Slide the omelette onto a plate and top one side with ice cream
and bananas. Drizzle with the sauce and flip the other side of the
omelette to enclose the filling. Dust with sugar and serve at once.

Goats' cheese and rocket omelette

For the omelette • 3 eggs • ¼ tsp fresh thyme leaves • 2 tbsp grated Parmesan cheese • 15g butter • For the filling • 6 cherry tomatoes, sliced • 6 pitted black olives, sliced • 75g mild soft goats' cheese • handful of rocket or baby spinach leaves, washed • 1 tsp vinaigrette dressing

SERVES 1–2

This savoury version of a soufflé omelette makes a really simple, light but delicious supper. With a topping of goats' cheese, tomatoes, rocket and olives, it has a real Mediterranean flavour to it.

1. Break 2 eggs into a bowl, separate the remaining egg and add the yolk to the eggs. Using an electric hand-held mixer, whisk the eggs until thick and foamy. Clean the beaters and whisk the egg white in a separate bowl until stiff.

2. Fold the egg white into the whisked eggs with the thyme leaves, Parmesan and some seasoning. Melt the butter in a small frying pan and pour in the egg mixture. Cook over a medium heat until golden underneath, 1–2 minutes.

3. Put the pan under a hot grill and grill until golden, 1 minute. Top one half with the tomato and olives then dot over spoonfuls of the goats' cheese. Toss the rocket in the dressing and add to the omelette. Flip over the uncovered half of the omelette and slide onto a plate.

batters

batters A batter at its simplest is a mixture based on flour and eggs that has a pouring consistency. Different batters serve different purposes: crepes, pancakes, griddle cakes and waffles are delicious served on their own or with sweet or savoury fillings or toppings, and variations on the batter mix can make a wealth of desserts or savoury snacks. Another use of batter is for coating foods before frying; fish or vegetables particularly benefit from this.

crepes the basic method Crepes are thin, frilly pancakes, made with a richer batter containing more eggs. If you want a fatter, fluffier pancake, follow the Griddle Cakes steps on page 116.

step 1 Sift the flour into a bowl with the salt and make a well in the centre. Break the eggs into the well and add a little of the milk. Gradually draw the flour in, then whisk well until smooth.

step 2 Add the remaining milk and whisk in gently until the batter is smooth with the consistency of light cream. Make sure you don't overwhip the batter at this stage.

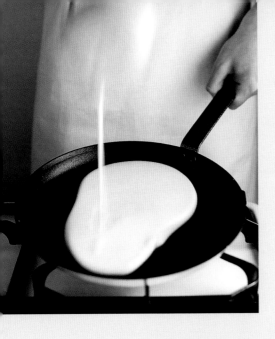

step 3 Heat a heavy-based or non-stick small frying pan or crepe pan and add a little of the clarified butter. Add a small ladleful of the batter and swirl around the base of the pan until evenly coated. Cook until golden, 1–2 minutes, then flip over and cook on the other side, another 1–2 minutes. Transfer to a plate. Repeat with the remaining mixture, adding a little more clarified butter between crepes until all the mixture is used up. The crepes can be reheated in the oven before serving.

Crepes suzette

100g plain flour • pinch salt • 2 large eggs • 300ml milk • clarified butter, for frying
For the orange butter • 100g butter • 2 tbsp icing sugar • 1 tbsp grated orange zest
To finish • 2 tbsp fresh orange juice • 3 tbsp brandy • 4 tbsp orange liqueur

SERVES 4

The classic French crepe recipe, this makes an impressive dinner party dessert, especially when you flambé the crepes in front of the guests.

1. Prepare the crepes following the steps above.

2. For the orange butter, soften the butter then whisk in the icing sugar and orange zest. Spread a little butter onto each crepe then return each in turn to a large frying pan, butter side down. Cook over a low heat until the butter has melted and the crepe is warmed through. Fold into quarters and slide to the side of the pan.

4. When all the crepes have been returned to the pan, pour over the orange juice and heat through.

5. Immediately before serving, pour on the brandy and orange liqueur. Light the sauce carefully with a long match, making sure all hair and clothing are kept away from the flame. Allow the flames to die down then serve with vanilla ice cream.

Summer berry crepes

For the crepes • 100g plain flour • pinch salt • 1 large egg • 300ml milk •
a few drops vanilla extract • 15g butter • 1 tbsp sunflower oil • For the fruit •
15g butter • 50g caster sugar • 1 tsp grated orange zest • 5 tbsp fresh orange juice •
350g mixed summer fruits, eg strawberries, raspberries, blueberries • 2 tbsp white rum •
1 tbsp icing sugar • whipped cream to serve • fresh fruit or mint leaves, to decorate

SERVES 4

Crepes make a wonderful dessert when teamed with seasonal fruits. These can be made ahead of time and reheated in the fruit and syrup in the pan.

1. Sift the flour into a bowl with the salt and make a well in the centre. Break in the egg and gradually add half the milk, whisking briskly to draw the flour into the egg.

2. Whisk in the remaining milk, vanilla extract and 4 tablespoons water to make a smooth batter which has the consistency of light cream.

3. Heat a small, non-stick frying pan and add the butter and oil. When the butter has melted, pour into a small bowl and return the pan to the heat. Add a small ladleful of the batter mixture and swirl around the base of the pan until evenly coated. Cook until golden then flip over and cook on the other side, 1–2 minutes in total. Slide the crepe onto a plate. Repeat with the remaining batter, adding a little of the butter and oil mixture between crepes.

4. For the fruit, melt the butter in a saucepan, stir in the sugar and cook gently for 1–2 minutes, until golden brown. Add the orange zest and juice and swirl the pan until the sugar has dissolved. Add the fruit and rum and cook until the fruit juices begin to run. Fold two crepes onto each serving plate and top with a spoonful of the fruit. Serve with cream and decorate with fresh fruit or mint.

Rich chocolate tarts

350g sweet shortcrust pastry • 100g plain chocolate • 2 eggs • 20g caster sugar • 150ml double cream

SERVES 6

These little tarts are filled with a wonderful chocolate batter that puffs up and just wobbles when it is cooked. Serve as a special treat with custard or cream.

1. Preheat the oven to 200°C/400°F/gas 6. Divide the pastry into six pieces. Roll out each piece thinly and use to line six individual tartlet tins. Chill 20 minutes. Prick the bases and line with baking parchment and baking beans. Bake blind, 15 minutes.

2. Remove the paper and beans and return to the oven an additional 5 minutes. Remove from the oven and set aside. Reduce the oven temperature to 190°C/375°F/gas 5.

3. Melt the chocolate in a bowl set over a pan of simmering water. Allow to cool slightly. Whisk the eggs and sugar in a bowl until pale. Whisk in the cream, then the melted chocolate. Pour the chocolate batter into the tartlet cases and bake until set, 15 minutes.

Cherry and almond clafoutis

25g butter • 450g black cherries • 25g plain flour • 50g icing sugar • 4 eggs • 250ml creamy milk • 2 tbsp kirsch • 2 tbsp flaked almonds

SERVES 4

1. Preheat the oven to 180°C/350°F/gas 4. Use the butter to grease a 1.2 litre dish. Scatter the cherries over the base.

2. Sift the flour and icing sugar together into a bowl and gradually whisk in the eggs until the mixture is smooth. Whisk in the milk and then stir in the kirsch.

3. Pour the batter over the cherries, then scatter over the flaked almonds. Bake until lightly set, 35–40 minutes. Cool slightly then dust with icing sugar before serving.

This is a classic recipe for clafoutis, a type of batter pudding, from the Limousin region of France where they grow cherries in abundance.

Burnt custard laced with bourbon

400ml double cream • 1 vanilla pod, split • 5 egg yolks • 100g caster sugar • 4 tbsp bourbon

SERVES 4

1. Preheat the oven to 200°C/400°F/gas 6. Heat the cream and vanilla pod over a low heat until almost boiling then leave to infuse 10 minutes. Whisk the egg yolks with 5 tablespoons of sugar until pale and thickened slightly. Stir in the hot cream and bourbon.

2. Pour into four 150ml ramekins and put them in a roasting tin. Pour in warm water to come half way up the sides. Bake until a skin has formed, but the custard is still wobbly, 12–15 minutes.

3. Chill the ramekins at least 3 hours. Scatter the remaining sugar over the tops. Cook under a hot grill or use a blow torch to caramelize the sugar. Let the caramel cool before serving.

This boozy version of a crème brûlée is truly out of this world. The custard should be lightly set in the middle with a thin, crisp, golden caramel on top.

Luxury blackcurrant pudding

8 medium thick slices of bread, crusts removed • 50g butter at room temperature •
225g fresh or frozen blackcurrants • 5 eggs • 75g caster sugar • 600ml creamy milk
(or even better, half milk and half double cream) • 2 tsp vanilla extract • freshly grated
nutmeg • 1 tbsp demerara sugar   **SERVES 4**

**Fresh blackcurrants add a refreshing tang to this
luxurious bread and butter pudding. Let the pudding
stand to cool for a while before eating or serve cold with
extra cream.**

1. Preheat the oven to 180°C/350°F/gas 4. Spread the bread with
the butter then cut diagonally in half. Generously butter a 2.2 litre
baking dish. Layer the bread slices in the dish, buttered side up,
scattering the blackcurrants between the layers as you go.

2. Whisk the eggs and sugar together lightly in a mixing bowl then
gradually whisk in the milk or milk and cream, the vanilla extract
and a large pinch of grated nutmeg.

3. Pour the batter over the bread, pushing the slices down well to
soak them thoroughly, scatter with the sugar and some more grated
nutmeg. Place the dish in a baking pan a quarter filled with hot
water. Bake until the top is crisp and golden, 1 hour.

4. Let cool slightly then serve with lightly whipped cream.

Griddle cakes

100g plain flour • 1 tsp bicarbonate of soda • ¾ tsp baking powder • 1 egg • 50g melted butter • 284ml carton buttermilk •100ml milk • To serve • 12 rashers streaky bacon • 50g baby spinach leaves • 150ml soured cream • ground black pepper, to garnish

SERVES 4

The batter for griddle pancakes has a thicker consistency and is lightened with a raising agent. Sweeten and serve as a dessert or, as here, they can be served as a savoury.

1. Sift the flour, bicarbonate of soda and baking powder into a bowl. Make a well in the centre and add the egg.

2. Add the butter, buttermilk and milk and whisk until smooth.

3. Heat a heavy-based frying pan or griddle. Wipe over a little oil then drop spoonfuls into the frying pan. Cook until bubbles appear on the surface and they are golden brown underneath. Quickly flip them over and cook until golden. Remove and keep warm.

4. Grill the bacon slices until crispy. Top a pile of griddle cakes with spinach leaves, the crisp cooked bacon and a spoonful of soured cream. Garnish with black pepper.

Pancakes with tropical fruit and maple syrup

100g plain flour • 1 tsp bicarbonate of soda • ¾ tsp baking powder • 1 tbsp sugar •
1 tsp vanilla extract • 1 egg, beaten • 50g melted butter • 284ml carton buttermilk •
oil for frying • 450g prepared mixed tropical fruits, eg pineapple, mango, papaya, kiwi,
cut into bite sized pieces • 250ml Greek or plain yogurt • maple syrup to drizzle

MAKES 12 pancakes

**These fluffy pancakes make an ideal brunch served
topped with fresh fruit, a spoonful of tangy yogurt and a
good drizzle of maple syrup. Alternatively, serve spread
with a little butter and a spoonful of fruit conserve for
afternoon tea.**

1. Sift the flour, bicarbonate of soda, baking powder and sugar into
a bowl. Add the vanilla extract, the egg, butter and buttermilk and
whisk until the mixture is smooth.

2. Heat a heavy-based frying pan or griddle. Wipe over a little oil
then drop spoonfuls into the frying pan. Cook until bubbles appear
on the surface and the pancakes are golden brown underneath. Flip
them over and cook until golden. Remove from the pan and keep
warm. Repeat with the remaining batter.

3. Combine the fruit in a bowl. Place three pancakes on each plate
and spoon some yogurt on top. Add some of the fruit and drizzle
with maple syrup before serving.

Peach, pecan and caramel waffles

For the waffles • 225g plain flour • 2 tsp baking powder • 1 tsp bicarbonate of soda • 2 eggs • 50g melted butter • 175ml milk • 284ml carton buttermilk • 1 tsp vanilla extract • To serve • 2 peaches • 75g pecan nuts, chopped • 1 tbsp light muscovado sugar • 5 tbsp maple syrup • 3 tbsp dark rum

MAKES 8-10 waffles

Waffles use a similar batter to the griddle cakes, but they have a little more raising agent and liquid – buttermilk or milk or a combination of the two.

1. First make the waffles. Sift the dry ingredients into a large bowl. Then whisk in the eggs, butter and milk, gradually incorporating the flour until smooth.

2. Add the buttermilk and vanilla extract to the mixture. Cover and let stand, 30 minutes. Heat a hand-held or electric waffle iron and pour a ladleful over two-thirds of the iron. Close it and wipe off any excess batter.

3. Cook 3–4 minutes, following the manufacturer's instructions.

4. When the batter stops steaming, open the iron and lift out the waffle with a fork. Keep hot in the oven.

5. Slice the peaches into wedges and spread over a baking tray. Scatter the pecans over the top and then sprinkle over the brown sugar. Drizzle with the maple syrup and dark rum and cook under a hot grill until the sugar is bubbling and the pecans are golden.

6. Spoon the peaches and pecans on top of the waffles and drizzle over some of the juices.

Corn cakes with prawn salsa

For the cakes • 100g plain flour • 1 tsp bicarbonate of soda • ¾ tsp baking powder • 1 large egg • 50g melted butter • 284ml carton buttermilk • 200g can sweetcorn, drained • **For the salsa** • 225g peeled prawns • ½ cucumber, peeled and diced • 6 tomatoes, diced • 1 red onion, quartered and finely sliced • 1 avocado, diced • 1 tbsp lime juice • 2 tbsp olive oil • a handful of fresh chopped coriander • 1 red chilli, finely chopped • salt and freshly ground black pepper

MAKES 12 cakes

Corn cakes accompany all types of food really well. Topped with this refreshing prawn salsa they make a wonderful lunch or supper.

1. Sift the flour, bicarbonate of soda and baking powder into a bowl. Add the egg, butter and buttermilk and whisk until smooth. Stir in the sweetcorn and set aside.

2. Heat a heavy-based frying pan or griddle. Wipe over a little oil then drop spoonfuls of the mixture into the pan. Spread out lightly to rough rounds then cook over a low heat until bubbles appear on the surface and they are dark golden brown underneath. Flip them over and cook until golden and firm to the touch. Remove from the pan and repeat with the remaining mixture.

3. Meanwhile make the salsa by combining everything in a bowl and mixing together well. Serve with the corn cakes.

Cheddar muffins

225 g cornmeal • 175g plain flour • 1 ½ tbsp baking powder • ½ tsp salt • 100g Cheddar cheese, grated • 1 small onion, grated • ¼ tsp chopped red chilli • 1 tbsp snipped fresh chives • 3 large eggs • 400ml milk • 100g melted butter

MAKES 12

Traditional American muffins are made with a thick batter but it shouldn't be overmixed or the muffins will be tough. All the mixing is done when you whisk the eggs and milk together. When the flour is gently folded in, the mixture will be very lumpy, but that is how it is supposed to be. These cheese and onion flavoured muffins make great savoury snacks to put in a packed lunch or can be served with soups, stews and casseroles. The mixture can be baked as a whole in a greased cake tin.

1. Preheat the oven to 200ºC/400ºF/gas 6. Line a 12-hole muffin tin with muffin papers and set aside. Sift the cornmeal, flour, baking powder and salt together in a bowl. Stir in the cheese, onion, chilli and chives. Use a balloon whisk to whisk the eggs, milk and butter together.

2. Stir the eggs, milk and butter into the flour mixture until combined but do not beat. It should still be quite lumpy.

3. Spoon the mixture into the muffin cases and bake until well risen, lightly golden and firm to the touch, 20 minutes. Serve warm.

Red snapper in crisp beer batter

100g plain flour • pinch salt • 2 eggs, separated • 1 tbsp groundnut oil • 200ml beer or ale • four 150g red snapper or trout fillets, halved • groundnut oil for deep frying • lemon slices, to serve

SERVES 4

The consistency of this batter can be varied by adding more or less liquid, in this case, beer. A runny consistency will produce a light, thin batter, and a thick one will cling better but be a bit more stodgy. Adding beaten egg whites makes it even lighter. Serve with fried potatoes and a green salad.

1. Sift the flour into a bowl and add the salt. Make a well in the centre and whisk in the egg yolks, oil and beer. Whisk until combined but still lumpy.

2. Leave to rest 30 minutes. Beat the egg whites in a mixing bowl until stiff and fold into the batter.

3. Heat the groundnut oil for deep frying to 190°C/375°F. Quickly dip two fish fillets into the batter, allowing the excess to drain back into the bowl. Gently lower into the oil and fry, turning often until the batter is golden, 2–3 minutes. Drain on paper towels and keep hot while frying the remaining fish. Serve with lemon slices.

Shrimp and vegetable tempura

1 egg • 250ml ice cold water • 75g plain flour, sifted • 50g cornflour • groundnut oil for deep frying • 225g raw tiger prawns, peeled and deveined • 1 courgette, thickly sliced • ½ small aubergine, cut into strips • 100g can baby corn, halved lengthwise • 1 large red pepper, deseeded and cut into thick strips • 2 small red onions, cut into wedges • To serve • 4 tbsp Japanese soy sauce • 1 spring onion, finely chopped • 1 red chilli, finely chopped

SERVES 4

Tempura batter is very light as it uses water rather than milk, and the water must be ice-cold. Here it coats a selection of vegetables and raw prawns but it's equally good with scallops and squid. Serve with a wedge of lemon if you prefer it to the Japanese-style dip.

1. Whisk the egg and ice-cold water together in a bowl. Sift the flours together then add to the egg mixture and whisk very briefly to combine. The lumps will keep the batter light when it's fried.

2. Heat the oil for deep-frying to 190°C/375°F. Dip a few prawns and pieces of the vegetables into the batter and add to the hot oil. Fry until lightly golden, 2–3 minutes. Remove with a slotted spoon and drain on paper towels. Fry the rest of the prawns and vegetables in the same way.

3. Mix the soy sauce with the spring onion and chilli and serve in a bowl with the prawns and vegetables.

sauces

sauces Many classic sauces are made using whisking techniques. Emulsified sauces like mayonnaise are made by whisking oil, egg yolks and vinegar, and in the case of aioli, by injecting garlic. Hollandaise and béarnaise sauces call for the same technique, but use butter instead of oil and are served hot. Use tasty butter sauces to enrich main courses by whisking butter into a reduction of wine, or create mouthwatering sweet sauces to top off desserts.

mayonnaise-style sauces the basic method

Mayonnaise and other emulsified sauces work best if the ingredients are at room temperature before you start. The usual ratio is 175ml oil per egg yolk.

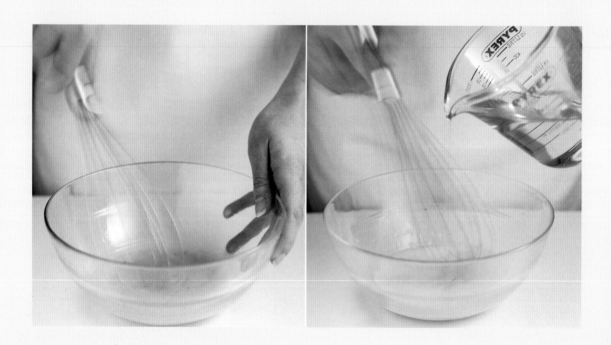

step 1 Using a balloon or egg whisk, whisk the egg yolks, seasoning, vinegar and mustard together until they thicken slightly. This should take about 1 minute.

step 2 Measure the oil into a measuring jug. Add the oil a drop at a time, whisking constantly. Keep whisking until it begins to thicken and lighten, after 2 tablespoons oil have been added.

step 3 Now you can start adding the oil more quickly. Continue whisking and add the oil in a thin steady stream, but not all at once, until the mixture is thick and glossy and holds its shape.

step 4 When all the oil has been added and whisked into the mayonnaise, taste it for seasoning, adding more salt and pepper if necessary, then stir in any flavouring ingredients.

Lemon herb mayonnaise with swordfish kebabs

For the mayonnaise • 1 egg yolk • 1 tbsp white wine vinegar • ½ tsp Dijon mustard • 200ml groundnut or light olive oil • salt and black pepper • **For the flavouring** • 2 tsp grated lemon zest • 1 tbsp chopped fresh tarragon • 1 tbsp chopped capers • 1 tbsp chopped fresh parsley • **For the kebabs** • 450g swordfish steaks, cut into bite-sized pieces • 2 red onions, cut into 6 wedges • 2 limes each cut into wedges • 2 tbsp olive oil • pared zest of 1 lime • 1 tsp fresh thyme leaves • 2 tbsp maple syrup

SERVES 4

All sorts of flavourings can be added to the basic mayonnaise. This lemon herb version goes really well with the swordfish kebabs.

1. For the mayonnaise, whisk the egg yolk, seasoning, vinegar and mustard together until they thicken slightly.

2. Add the oil a drop at a time whisking constantly. When the sauce begins to thicken and lighten, start adding the oil in a thin, steady stream, whisking constantly.

3. When all the oil has been added, taste for seasoning then stir in the lemon zest, tarragon, capers and parsley. Set aside.

4. Put the swordfish, red onion and lime wedges into a bowl and toss in the oil, lime zest, thyme leaves and maple syrup. Chill 2–3 hours. Thread the fish, lime wedges and red onion onto eight skewers and cook under a hot grill 5–6 minutes, turning often until starting to colour on the outside. Serve the kebabs with a spoonful of the sauce, new potatoes and a side salad.

Note: Recipes using raw eggs should be avoided by infants, the elderly, pregnant women and anyone with a compromised immune system.

Tomato and olive salad with basil mayonnaise

For the mayonnaise • **1 egg yolk** • **salt and black pepper** • **2 tsp balsamic vinegar** •
1 tsp Dijon mustard • **100ml groundnut oil** • **2 tsp pesto sauce** • **pinch of sugar** •
For the salad • **2 beefsteak tomatoes, sliced thickly** • **175g yellow cherry tomatoes,**
halved • **175g baby plum tomatoes, halved** • **10cm piece cucumber, peeled and sliced** •
1 red onion, thinly sliced • **handful rocket leaves** • **100g feta cheese, crumbled** •
75g mixed marinated olives

SERVES 4

**These three ingredients work really well together and
topped with tangy feta cheese make the perfect salad for
a summer lunch. Make sure the tomatoes are at room
temperature to bring out their flavour.**

1. For the basil mayonnaise, whisk the egg yolk, seasoning,
1 teaspoon vinegar and mustard together until they thicken slightly.

2. Whisk in the oil a drop at a time. When the sauce begins to
thicken and lighten – after about 1 tablespoon of the oil has been
added – add the oil in a steady stream, whisking constantly.

3. When all the oil has been added, stir in the remaining vinegar.
Season then add the pesto and sugar and set aside.

4. Combine all the tomatoes on a large platter. Scatter over the
cucumber, onion, rocket, feta and olives. Serve with a spoonful of
the basil mayonnaise and warm bread.

Note: Recipes using raw eggs should be avoided by infants, the elderly, pregnant
women and anyone with a compromised immune system.

Salmon and dill cakes with hollandaise sauce

For the salmon cakes • 200g raw tiger prawns, peeled • 450g skinned salmon fillet, finely chopped • 1 tbsp drained capers, chopped • 2 tbsp chopped fresh dill • 2 spring onions, finely chopped • 2 tsp grated lemon zest • 25g fresh white breadcrumbs • For the hollandaise • 175g butter • 3 egg yolks • 1 tbsp fresh lemon juice

SERVES 4

The key to a good hollandaise sauce is gentle heat and plenty of whisking. The resulting sauce should be a stable creamy emulsion of egg yolks and butter, flavoured with either a reduction of vinegar, wine or, more commonly, lemon juice. Serve while still warm.

1. First make the salmon cakes. Blend the prawns in a food processor to a paste. Put into a bowl with the salmon fillet, capers, dill, spring onions, lemon zest, seasoning and breadcrumbs. Shape into small cakes and chill at least 1 hour before using.

2. Melt the butter in a saucepan over a low heat. Remove from the heat and let cool slightly. Put 2 tablespoons water and the egg yolks in a bowl and set over a saucepan of gently simmering water. Season and whisk until the yolks form a pale, thick mousse that leaves a ribbon trail on the surface for 5 seconds.

3. Gradually pour in the melted butter, whisking constantly. Discard any white, milky sediment left in the bottom of the butter pan.

4. Whisk in the lemon juice and season to taste. If the consistency is too thick, add a little boiling water, a spoonful at a time, until the required consistency is reached.

5. Cook the salmon cakes on a hot oiled griddle, 8–10 minutes. Serve with an avocado and tomato salad with a spoonful of the hollandaise sauce on the side.

Grilled prawns with aioli

For the aioli • 1 egg yolk • 2 garlic cloves • ½ tsp Dijon mustard • 1 tbsp fresh lemon juice • pinch sugar • 150ml light olive oil • To serve • 12 fresh asparagus spears, about 250g • 12 large raw tiger prawns • oil for brushing • pinch of ground paprika, to garnish • freshly chopped parsley, to garnish

SERVES 4

Aioli is a wonderful garlicky sauce that goes well with all types of foods, but especially well with fish and asparagus. Serve with grilled vegetables or serve with burgers instead of mayonnaise.

1. Place the egg yolk, garlic, mustard, lemon juice, sugar and seasoning in a bowl and whisk together briefly.

2. Gradually whisk in the oil until thick and glossy, then chill until required.

3. Blanch the asparagus spears in boiling salted water, 3 minutes. Drain and put in a bowl of cold water to stop the spears from overcooking.

4. Heat a large griddle pan or barbecue, brush the prawns with oil and cook, 2–3 minutes each side. Set aside. Cook the asparagus spears in the same way, until lightly charred, 1–2 minutes. Garnish with paprika and parsley and serve with the aioli sauce.

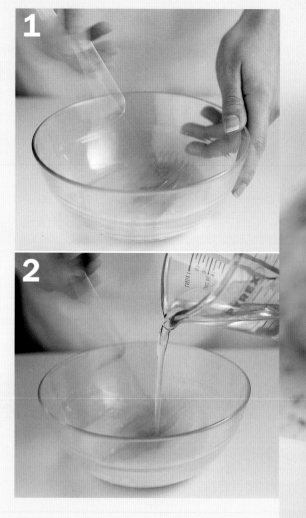

Note: Recipes using raw eggs should be avoided by infants, the elderly, pregnant women and anyone with a compromised immune system.

Thyme and orange chicken with herb butter sauce

For the sauce • **1 tbsp white wine** • **2 tbsp white wine vinegar** • **1 shallot, finely chopped** • **1 tbsp double cream** • **100g very cold butter, cubed** • **For the flavouring** • **1 tsp snipped chives** • **2 tsp torn basil leaves** • **For the chicken** • **4 chicken breasts, skinned and boned** • **2 tbsp olive oil** • **1 tsp fresh thyme leaves** • **2 garlic cloves, crushed** • **2 tsp grated orange zest** • **1 tbsp fresh orange juice** • **1 tbsp clear honey**

SERVES 4

Butter sauces are made by vigorously whisking small pieces of very cold butter into a wine and vinegar reduction over gentle heat until a smooth emulsion is formed. The aim is to melt the butter into a creamy emulsion rather than letting it become an oil that floats on the surface of the sauce. Often served with grilled fish or white meat.

1. Make the herb butter sauce. Boil the wine, vinegar and shallots in a small heavy-based pan until most of the liquid has evaporated.

2. Add the cream and reduce a little. Use a spiral whisk to whisk the butter a cube at a time into the mixture in the saucepan. Do not allow the sauce to boil.

3. Season to taste and stir in the chives and basil.

4. Put the chicken breasts into a shallow dish and score them with a sharp knife. Add the oil, thyme leaves, garlic, orange zest and juice, honey and seasoning. Mix together well. Grill the chicken on a rack under a hot grill, turning once until lightly golden, 8–10 minutes. Serve the chicken with fresh green vegetables, boiled new potatoes and a spoonful of the butter sauce.

1

Egg florentine with beurre rouge

For the sauce • 90ml red wine • 2 shallots, finely chopped • 1 tbsp crème fraiche •
225g very cold butter • 1 tsp sun-dried tomato paste • To serve • 15g butter • 1 garlic
clove, crushed • 675g baby leaf spinach, washed • 4 large fresh eggs

SERVES 4

This variation of a classic French butter sauce is made
with a reduction of red wine. It is perfect to serve with
poached eggs or over vegetables but is also good
spooned over peeled grilled prawns or fish. Serve with
toasted ciabatta bread.

1. To make the red butter sauce, boil the wine and shallots in a
small heavy-based saucepan until 1 tablespoon of the liquid
remains. Add the crème fraiche and reduce a little. Whisk in the
butter, a cube at a time, letting each piece melt into the mixture
before adding the next. Season to taste and stir in the tomato
purée. Set aside.

2. Heat the butter for the spinach in a saucepan and add the
garlic. Cook 1 minute then add the spinach, cover and allow to wilt,
1–2 minutes.

3. Break the eggs into a pan of boiling water and poach until the
whites are firm but yolks are still soft, 3–4 minutes. Drain the
spinach and spoon onto serving plates. Top with a drained egg and
spoon over a little red butter sauce. Grind some black pepper over
the top before serving.

Provençal beef with béarnaise dressing

For the béarnaise • 175g butter • 3 tbsp white wine vinegar • 3 tbsp white wine
10 peppercorns • 3 shallots, finely chopped • 1 tbsp chopped fresh tarragon • 3 egg
yolks • 1 tbsp fresh chopped mixed chives and parsley • For the beef • 675g sirloin
steak • 200g fine green beans, trimmed and blanched • 3 beefsteak tomatoes, cut into
chunky pieces • 400g can butter beans • 75g pitted black olives

SERVES 4

A béarnaise sauce is another version of an emulsified sauce with a more pungent flavour. It goes really well with beef or lamb steak.

1. First make the sauce. Melt the butter in a saucepan over a low heat. Remove from the heat and allow to cool slightly. Pour the vinegar and wine into a pan and add the peppercorns, shallots and tarragon. Bring to a boil and cook until reduced to about 1 tablespoon of liquid. Add 1 tablespoon water to cool the mixture slightly then strain into a bowl.

2. Add the egg yolks to the bowl and set over a saucepan of gently simmering water. Season, then whisk until pale and thick or until the whisk leaves a trail on the surface of the mixture for 5 seconds.

3. Gradually pour in the melted butter, whisking constantly, leaving any white, milky sediment at the bottom of the butter saucepan. Pour through a sieve and stir in the chives and parsley.

4. Heat a griddle pan. Season the steak and cook to your liking, 5–8 minutes each side. Meanwhile combine the green beans, tomatoes, butter beans and olives with some seasoning. Remove the steak from the griddle and set aside. Add the vegetables to the hot griddle and cook until heated through, 2 minutes. Divide between four plates. Carve the steak and serve on top of the warm salad with some warm béarnaise sauce drizzled over the top.

Vanilla poached plums with custard

For the custard • 300ml creamy milk • ½ vanilla pod, split • 3 egg yolks • 40g caster sugar • ¾ tsp cornflour • **For the plums** • 50g caster sugar • ½ vanilla pod, split • 450g red plums, halved and stoned

SERVES 4

It's helpful to know when making custard that the basic proportions are 1 egg yolk to 100ml creamy milk. Adding ¼ teaspoon cornflour per egg yolk will stabilize the custard. After initial whisking, switch to a wooden spoon to stir the custard – you want a creamy consistency rather than a frothy one.

1. Cook the plums. Put the sugar, 175ml water and the vanilla pod in a saucepan. Bring slowly to a boil, stirring until the sugar has dissolved. Boil 2 minutes then add the plums, cover and cook gently until tender, 3–5 minutes. Remove from the heat and set aside.

2. For the custard, pour the milk into a saucepan and add the vanilla pod. Bring slowly to a boil, turn off the heat and let infuse, 10 minutes. Remove the vanilla pod.

3. Whisk the egg yolks, sugar and cornflour together until thick and lightened. Whisk in the hot milk. Return to a clean heavy-based saucepan and heat gently, stirring all the time until the custard is almost at boiling point and has thickened slightly.

4. Plunge the base of the pan in a bowl of cold water for a few seconds to stop the custard from over-cooking. Spoon the plums into glass bowls and pour some of the custard over the top.

Grilled bananas with chocolate sauce

For the chocolate sauce • 300ml creamy milk • ½ vanilla pod, split • 3 egg yolks • 40g caster sugar • ¾ tsp cornflour (optional) • 50g plain chocolate, grated • To serve • 4 bananas • 15g butter • 3 tbsp caster sugar • 4 slices panettone

SERVES 4

This chocolate sauce can be served over any fruit but it goes particularly well with grilled bananas. Try it with poached pears and vanilla ice cream on the panettone for an equally delicious variation.

1. For the chocolate sauce, pour the milk into a saucepan and add the vanilla pod. Bring slowly to the boil, turn off the heat and let infuse, 10 minutes. Remove the vanilla pod.

2. Whisk the egg yolks, sugar and cornflour together until pale and slightly thickened. Gradually whisk in the hot milk.

3. Return to a clean heavy-based saucepan and heat, gently stirring all the time until the custard is at boiling point and has thickened. Remove from the heat and stir in the chocolate until melted.

4. Heat a griddle pan. Slice the bananas in half lengthwise then in half into four shorter pieces. Dip the long cut side in the butter and then the sugar. Place on the griddle cut side down and cook until the bananas are lightly browned, 1–2 minutes. Turn over and cook another 30 seconds. Remove from the griddle. Repeat with the panettone, until it is warmed through.

5. Place the panettone on plates and top with the bananas. Drizzle with the chocolate custard to serve.

index

aioli: Grilled prawns with aioli 134
almonds:
 Almond macaroons 64
 Apricot and almond soufflé omelette 102
 Cherry and almond clafoutis 114
 Orange and almond sponge cake 30
 Simple almond cake 45
amaretti: Plum and amaretti sponge cake slice 36
American sponge: the basic method 16-17
American whipped sponge cake 18
Angel food cake 42
 the basic method 40-41
apples: Apple and Calvados soufflé 94
Apricot and almond omelette 102

bananas:
 Butterscotch, pecan, and banana soufflé omelette 104
 Grilled bananas with chocolate sauce 142
basil: Tomato and olive salad with basil mayonnaise 132
batters 108
béarnaise sauce 128, 139
beef: Provençal beef with béarnaise dressing 139
berries:
 Cherry and berry roulade 101
 Mixed berry basket 55
 Summer berry crepes 110
 see also individual berries
blackcurrants:
 Black currant and white rum fool 75
 Luxury black currant pudding 115
blackberries: Classic cheesecake with blackberry topping 38
Blue lagoon ice cream 72
blueberries:
 Blue lagoon ice cream 72
 Blueberry and white chocolate meringue roll 67
brownies: Double chocolate chunk brownies 34
Burnt custard laced with bourbon 114
butter:
 Egg florentine with beurre rouge 138
 Thyme and orange chicken with herb butter sauce 136
Butterscotch, pecan, and banana

soufflé omelette 104
Candied fruit bombe 77
Candied fruit cassata 20
Cappuccino truffle cake 46
caramel:
 Peach, pecan, and caramel waffles 119
 Tropical caramel meringues 54
Caribbean coconut trifle 78
cassata: Candied fruit cassata 20
cheese:
Cheddar muffins 122
Cheese soufflé 92
Goats' cheese and rocket omelette 105
cheesecake: Classic cheesecake with blackberry topping 38
cherries:
 Cherry and almond clafoutis 114
 Cherry and berry roulade 101
 Cherry syllabub 87
 Coconut and cherry Swiss roll 26
chicken: Thyme and orange chicken with herb butter sauce 136
Chilled mandarin and lemon mousse 82
chocolate:
 Blueberry and white chocolate meringue roll 67
 Cappuccino truffle cake 46
 Chocolate and chestnut macaroon cake 63
 Chocolate and raspberry torte 23
 Devil's food cake with chocolate orange frosting 33
 Double chocolate chunk brownies 34
 Double chocolate mini alaskas 58
 Festive chocolate and hazelnut roulade 100
 Grilled bananas with chocolate sauce 142
 Kahlua and chocolate trifle 79
 Rich chocolate tarts 113
 Rich mocha pots 83
Classic cheesecake with blackberry topping 38
coconut:
 Caribbean coconut trifle 78
 Coconut and cherry Swiss roll 26
coffee:
 Cappuccino truffle cake 46
 Coffee and maple ice cream 74
 Coffee, maple, and pecan sponge cake 21
 Rich mocha pots 83
Corn cakes with prawn salsa 120
cottage cheese: Curd cheese tarts 39
creamed sponge cake: the basic

method 28-9
Creamy zabaglione 84
crepes 108-9
 Crepes suzette 109
 Summer berry crepes 110
Curd cheese tarts 39
custard:
 Burnt custard laced with bourbon 114
 Vanilla poached plums with custard 141

Devil's food cake with chocolate orange frosting 33
Double chocolate chunk brownies 34
Double chocolate mini alaskas 58

eggs: Egg florentine with beurre rouge 138
 egg whites, whisking 8-9

Festive chocolate and hazelnut roulade 100
fish see individual types of fish
folding 17, 18, 21, 23, 24, 26-30, 32, 33, 34, 36, 38, 41, 42, 44, 45, 52, 55, 59, 62, 78, 84, 91, 94, 95, 97, 100, 101, 102, 104, 105, 109, 122
fruit:
 Candied fruit bombe 77
 Candied fruit cassata 20
 Pancakes with tropical fruit and maple syrup 118
 Seared fruit in frothy orange sauce 86
 see also individual fruits

garlic: Mushroom and garlic soufflé 95
Goats' cheese and rocket omelette 105
Griddle cakes 116
Grilled bananas with chocolate sauce 142
Grilled prawns with aioli 134

hazelnuts:
 Festive chocolate and hazelnut roulade 100
 Hazelnut meringue cake 59
herbs:
 Lemon herb mayonnaise with swordfish kebabs 131
 Thyme and orange chicken with herb butter sauce 136
hollandaise sauce 128
 Salmon and dill cakes with hollandaise sauce 133
ice cream:
 the basic method 70-71
 Blue lagoon ice cream 72

Coffee and maple ice cream 74
Strawberry ice cream angel cake 44

Kahlua and chocolate trifle 79

lemons:
Chilled mandarin and lemon
mousse 82
Lemon and poppy seed pound cake
32
Lemon herb mayonnaise with
swordfish kebabs 131
Lemon-lime meringue pie 60
Swiss roll with lemon cream
24
limes:
Frosted lime tray-bake 35
Lemon-lime meringue pie 60
Luxury blackcurrant pudding 115
Lychee sorbet 80

macaroons: Almond macaroons 64
mandarin oranges: Chilled mandarin
and lemon mousse 82
maple syrup:
Coffee and maple ice cream 74
Coffee, maple, and pecan sponge
cake 21
Pancakes with tropical fruit and
maple syrup 118
mayonnaise:
Grilled prawn with aioli 134
Lemon herb mayonnaise with
swordfish kebabs 131
mayonnaise-style sauces: the basic
method 128-9
Tomato and olive salad with basil
mayonnaise 132
meringue 8, 11, 13, 45, 50, 60
Blueberry and white chocolate
meringue roll 67
Chocolate and chestnut macaroon
cake 63
Double chocolate mini alaskas 58
fingers 51
Hazelnut meringue cake 59
Lemon-lime meringue pie 601
Meringue nests 51, 52
Mixed berry basket 55
quenelles 51
Raspberry and passionfruit pavlova
57
Strawberry and pistachio vacherin
62
Tropical caramel meringues 54
Middle Eastern orange cake 27
Mixed berry basket 55
muffins: Cheddar muffins 122
mushrooms: Mushroom and garlic
soufflé 95

omelettes:
Apricot and almond soufflé omelette
102
Butterscotch, pecan, and banana
soufflé omelette 104
Goats' cheese and rocket omelette
105
oranges:
Chilled mandarin and lemon
mousse 82
Devil's food cake with chocolate
orange frosting 33
Middle Eastern orange cake 27
Orange and almond sponge cake 30
Thyme and orange chicken with
herb butter sauce 136

Pancakes with tropical fruit and maple
syrup 118
passionfruit: Raspberry and
passionfruit pavlova 57
Peach, pecan, and caramel waffles
119
plums:
Plum and amaretti sponge cake
slice 36
Vanilla poached plums with custard
141
poppy seeds: Lemon and poppy seed
pound cake 32
prawns:
Corn cakes with prawn salsa 120
Grilled prawn with aioli 134
Prawn and vegetable tempura 125
Provençal beef with béarnaise
dressing 139

quenelles 51

raspberries:
Chocolate and raspberry torte 23
Raspberry and passionfruit pavlova
57
Red snapper in crisp beer batter 124
ribbon stage 24
Rich chocolate tarts 113
Rich mocha pots 83
rocket: Goat's cheese and rocket
omelette 105
roulades:
Cherry and berry roulade 101
Festive chocolate and hazelnut
roulade 100
Spinach roulade 98
rum: Blackcurrant and white rum fool
75

salads: Tomato and olive salad with
basil mayonnaise 132
Salmon and dill cakes with
hollandaise sauce 133

salsa: Corn cakes with prawn salsa
120
sauces 128
béarnaise 128, 139
butter 11, 128
chocolate 142
cream 11
egg-based 11
emulsified 128
hollandaise 128, 133
mayonnaise 128-9, 131, 132, 134
sweet 128
Seared fruit in frothy orange sauce
86
Simple almond cake 45
soufflés 90-91
Apple and Calvados soufflé 94
Cheese soufflé 92
Mushroom and garlic soufflé 95
Sweet vanilla soufflé 97
spinach:
Egg florentine with beurre rouge
138
Spinach roulade 98
sponge cake:
American sponge: the basic
method 16-17
creamed sponge cake: the basic
method 28-9
Swiss roll with lemon cream
24
strawberries:
Strawberry and pistachio vacherin
62
Strawberry ice cream angel cake 44
Summer berry crepes 110
Sweet vanilla soufflé 97
swordfish: Lemon herb mayonnaise
with swordfish kebabs 131

tempura: Shrimp and vegetable
tempura 125
Thyme and orange chicken with herb
butter sauce 136
tomatoes: Tomato and olive salad with
basil mayonnaise 132
Tropical caramel meringues 54

vanilla:
Sweet vanilla soufflé 97
Vanilla poached plums with custard
141

waffles: Peach, pecan, and caramel
waffles 119
whipping 6, 7-8, 28-9, 40-1, 70-1,
90-1, 128-29

zabaglione: Creamy zabaglione 84